Date Due

161

Mody Boatright, Folklorist

A COLLECTION OF ESSAYS

Mody Boatright, 1896–1970

Mody Boatright, Folklorist

A COLLECTION OF ESSAYS

Edited with an Introduction by ERNEST B. SPECK

Biographical Essay by HARRY H. RANSOM

FOREWORD BY WAYLAND D. HAND

PUBLISHED FOR THE *Texas Folklore Society* BY THE
UNIVERSITY OF TEXAS PRESS · AUSTIN & LONDON

Library of Congress Cataloging in Publication Data

Boatright, Mody Coggin. 1896–1970.
    Mody Boatright, folklorist: a collection of essays:

    Bibliography: p.
    1. Folk-lore—The West—Addresses, essays, lectures.
2. Folk-lore—Texas—Addresses, essays, lectures.
3. Boatright, Mody Coggin, 1896–1970.   I. Speck,
Ernest B., ed.   II. Texas Folklore Society.
III. Title.
GR109.B52   398.2′32′76   73-6908
ISBN 0-292-75007-2

Composition by G&S Typesetters, Austin
Printing by The University of Texas Printing Division, Austin
Binding by Universal Bookbindery, Inc., San Antonio

CONTENTS

Foreword vii
    Wayland D. Hand

Biographical Essay xi
    Harry H. Ransom

Introduction xix
    Ernest B. Speck

Acknowledgments xxv

1. The Genius of Pecos Bill (1929) . . . 3
2. The Myth of Frontier Individualism (1941) . 13
3. Frontier Humor: Despairing or Buoyant? (1942) . 39
4. Gib Morgan among the Heroes (1945) . . 61
5. The Art of Tall Lying (1949) 68
6. The American Myth Rides the Range:
    Owen Wister's Man on Horseback (1951) . 80
7. Aunt Cordie's Ax and Other Motifs in Oil (1953) . 92
8. On the Nature of Myth (1954) 106
9. Folklore in a Literate Society (1958) . . 116
10. The Family Saga as a Form of Folklore (1958) . 124
11. The Oil Promoter as Trickster (1961) . . . 145
12. Theodore Roosevelt, Social Darwinism,
    and the Cowboy (1964) 163

13. How Will Boatright Made Bits and Spurs (1970) .   179

Selected Bibliography   187
Index   191

FOREWORD

At a time when profound changes are taking place in the study of folklore in America and when traditional approaches to the subject are being seriously challenged and often found wanting according to the scholarly canons of a new generation of workers, it is instructive to assess the contribution to our discipline of the late Mody C. Boatright. An inquiry into his work is facilitated with the publication of a series of his essays on folklore and related subjects, drawn together in this memorial volume by one of Boatright's students, Ernest B. Speck. Dr. Speck is professor of English at Sul Ross State University, where Mody Boatright began his own professorial career in 1923, when Sul Ross was a small teachers college.

Having been a member of the Texas Folklore Society for many years and having met John A. Lomax and J. Frank Dobie in the 1940s and many other members of the Society since that time, I am afraid that I do not have all the scholarly detachment that might be expected of one so remote from Texas as a Californian. I first became interested in the history of the Texas Folklore Society in 1943. As I came to know the people who had launched and sustained the most successful state and regional folklore society in the country, I wondered what the compelling forces were that helped to maintain the collection and study of folklore with such unabated zeal in Texas when just about everywhere else in the country there were ups and downs in state and local folklore enterprises, and many casualties along the way that could only be laid at the door of indifference or adverse circumstance. It was not until 1966, however, when I went to Austin to address the Society on "The Eyes of Texas: Fifty Years of Folklore in the Southwest," that I came to understand the motivating forces within the Society and the members who made for such sound growth and endurance. The answer was simple enough: a love of the land and its people and a pride in the Lone Star State that could, seemingly, only be sustained and nourished by continually adding to the body of myth and legend that this love itself had engendered.

As a loyal native son of Texas, Boatright came by his pride in the state and its people easily enough, but this devotion to Texas life and to the Texian spirit and outlook did not bind him to a parochial view of the world about him. Boatright was a free and independent spirit who saw Texas in a broader regional setting than many others and who likewise tried to view Texas and the Southwest in proper historical perspective and to judge its people in terms of American character in general as well as regional types encountered in other parts of a burgeoning America. In reading, and in some cases rereading, the essays in the present volume, I am struck by Boatright's fine knowledge of America's cultural development. There is maturity in his judgments that is invariably tempered by reference to the lessons of history and guided by the insights afforded by the social sciences. He looked on both as needed adjuncts to his fields of specialty in American letters and American folklore.

His knowledge of America's past, acquired over many years in a conscious broadening of background for his specialities, made it unnecessary for Boatright to employ the cant and jargon of his métier to enforce narrow interpretations or to plead a special point of view. On the contrary, since almost all of his professional writing was directed to an informed general public, he developed a clear and forceful expository style that was sharpened by many years' experience as editor and critic. To this practical scholarly endowment he brought the expressive beauty and grace of a born creative writer. Among folklorists of his day, Boatright's skill and penetration at literary and critical levels have rarely been surpassed.

It is too soon, of course, to judge the final impact of Boatright's contributions to folklore in his own part of the country or in the broader arena. While these works will likely not escape the attacks launched upon the whole scholarly legacy of the founders of folklore study both abroad and of his own generation here at home, the Boatright corpus will stand. It will stand because it constitutes a unique contribution to our knowledge of folklife in Texas and the Southwest. It will stand, moreover, because it is historically sound in terms of America's cultural development, because it is innately honest, and because it avoids pretense in statement and is free of "scholarly" manipulation. Finally, it will stand because its appeal is eminently humane and decent— a contribution worthy of such a great human being as Mody Coggin Boatright.

WAYLAND D. HAND

University of California
Los Angeles, California

MODY BOATRIGHT, 1896–1970

In the terse record provided the University of Texas by Mody Boatright in annual departmental reports, many of the most important facts about him are missing. Only memory among those who knew him and legend among those who did not can fill out the story—his resolute principles and redoubtable courage, his honesty and candor, his patience and tolerance, his clearly reasoned beliefs and his suspension of hard reasoning on behalf of those who were handicapped or dismally beset by circumstance.

Adjectives used to describe Mody as a man include "gentle," "fair," "quiet," "loyal," "friendly." All these words are apt. Yet beyond mere verbal description there were other qualities evident to those who were his friends. He had suffered and knew how to endure suffering with courage and grace. On what seemed to him to be essential principles, he was immovably strong.

Mody's earliest formal education was made up of successive tutorial courses at home. A year's service in the army interrupted his plans for study. In 1922 he received the A.B. degree from West Texas State Teachers College. The following year, the University of Texas conferred on him the A.M. in English. He completed his doctoral work at Texas in 1932.

After a brief term of teaching at Sul Ross State Teachers College, Mody was appointed instructor of English in the University at Austin in 1926. From that time until his retirement in 1968—with the exception of one year at the College of Mines—he was a member of the University faculty. He served in all the English Department's academic ranks, from junior instructor to chairman.

As a professor and professional folklorist, Mody was a member of the Executive Committee and a fellow of the American Folklore Society, editor or joint editor of numerous publications of the Texas Folklore Society, and an interested participant in the work of American Studies groups, the South Central Modern Language Association, the Texas Institute of Letters, dialect societies, and a few congenial clubs, which as he once said "sometimes make good talk even when they do not make sense."

Because he influenced the interpretation of the state, some acquaintances have called Mody a "typical Texan." In any context, however, he would have stayed individual. Hence he brought to his interpretation of Texan themes a mixture of enthusiasm and keen insight that had nothing to do with either false pride in a region or defensive provincialism.

In that interpretation, some of his most serious studies were made during the heyday of the Texas "brags and boasts." Unlike those southwesterners who declaim contradiction or print diatribe whenever disagreement moves them, Mody took both idiotic and well-reasoned comment with equal calm. Twisting facts to turn a colorful anecdote, however, roused in him instant response. When George Lyman Kittredge visited an evangelical prayer meeting near Austin, somebody manufactured a fanciful yarn concluded by the suggestion that the congregation thought that Kittredge was Moses. Having received a long "folklore" anecdote to that effect, Mody wrote across the face of the manuscript: "Nonsense. The congregation thought Kittredge was a white-haired professor from Harvard."

The gathering-in of manuscripts for a volume to be called *Mustangs and Cow Horses* turned up numerous alliterative titles. One headed an awkward plagiarism of the widely published legend of the pacing white mustang. The paper was called "Pegasus of the Plains." Boatright dismissed it with a note: "Reject. Pegasus never got this far west." I think a different kind of fabrication, called "Jet-Tailed Jenny," appealed to him a little. But he stuck by knowledge in his editorial rejection: "Jennies were better known for endurance and devotion than they were for speed. Get somebody to write about the Air Corps Jenny; then neither anachronism nor the m.p.h. will count."

If Mody had a permanent editorial soft spot, it was his sympathy with men and women who had worked with their hands —or as he once put it, "with their hands and their feet and their hearts." He could get excited about the prospect of an account by an old-time horse wrangler or roustabout from the oil-boom era. For a volume to contain such reminiscences he suggested, "It's all right for us to celebrate the dignity of labor; but it's more important for this series to catch the sense of personal identity felt by the worker and his delight in accomplishment of a job."

Such feelings, of course, were more likely to get into conversation than into writing. That was why Mody was one of the first of the oral historians. His archive on the Texas oil industry was begun long before "oral history" became a subject of discussion at learned meetings. The archive stands as a major accomplishment. "You can't sing it, like the Lomaxes' great collection," he wrote, "but it does have the rhythm of daily life and sometimes a phrase that is inspired."

In the Boatright era, we saw swift transitions, new departures, subtle changes. Among all of them, Mody was highly adaptable. Some educators adapt by whirling like an academic windsock. Not Mody. His changing came out of qualities of character—

lively human interest, deep human sympathy. His altruism was neither polite sentiment nor professional expediency. "He is sincerely interested in other people—what they think, what they are doing, what they hope to do." That opinion came from one of Mody's students in the thirties. It applied to his whole University life. It stayed true, and it is worth emphasis when we consider the scarcity of his kind.

I do not mean that Mody put empty amiability above serious argument. He did not retreat to vague agreeableness in order to avoid collision of ideas. On the contrary, he knew that friction is inevitable and can be healthful.

Recent decades have found new academic voices, new idioms. During that time, nobody doubted that Mody knew when to express an opinion. He never got to his feet just to be heard; hence the power of his opinion when it was expressed.

English Department minutes are scanty. That is just as well. Set down verbatim, they would have made heavier poundage than those of the general faculty. One instance will do to reflect Mody's influence. Frank Dobie did not adopt opinions secondhand without reason. At one interminable meeting of the department (at which Dobie, as usual, arrived late), argument had moved in circles. When Frank settled down in the back of the room, he asked quite audibly, "Has Mody talked yet?" He got an affirmative answer. Whereupon Frank rose, shook his mane, and told the department, "Well, I second whatever it was that Mody said before I came in and call for the question."

No matter how hot the argument or perplexed the issue, Mody was never intentionally unkind or unfair to any student or colleague. Since its founding there have been few members of the University whose lives inspired the kind of personal loyalty and those many kinds of personal trust which his integrity and gentle wisdom enlisted among those of us who studied and worked with him.

His deep concern about the human being was an essential

part of his personal life. It also guided actions taken officially. Before World War II, he was asked to comment on a report concerning students admitted to the University with low high-school grades. His position was quite clear:

> My comments on the reports concerning "students from the fourth quartile" will seem negative. I intend them to be constructive.
>
> In the first place, this is a questionable label to those who understand it and a meaningless one to those who don't. To dub students "bottom-of-their-class" graduates even temporarily does nothing to clarify their problems or spur their achievement. Graduating classes inside and outside Texas differ vastly; to be in the lowest ten percent of some classes may mean as much as being at the top of others. More important, there are all kinds of reasons why a student may graduate at low rank.
>
> The really important problem is defined by other reports and new programs at Texas which emphasize the individual student's experience, objectives, abilities, and personal conceptions of his education. [It has been pointed out that] some of our most distinguished alumni fall in this category of low-rank entrance (some actually were admitted on special approval). There are many faculty members who would be willing to work hard with such people. If I am wrong there, then we should get teachers who are interested. In any case, the SFTFQ report should be buried in the files—or burned.
>
> I do not suggest substituting a come-one, come-all program. I do think that those departments which a freshman student is likely to meet when he reaches the campus should look once at what he did in high school and then get on with the job of helping him do the best he can in college.

A strong suggestion in the 1950s that the abilities of some women on the University faculty had not received practical recognition drew Mody's instant support. Married to one of the truly talented artists of the Southwest, Elizabeth Keefer Boatright, he was intensely proud of her work. That his sense of fairness went beyond close relationship is demonstrated by this note: "The way to get at recognition of women on this faculty is to quit considering it a problem. Advancement, including promotion, should be based solely on merit. So I'd say we don't need another 'study' or 'program.' What we need is a visible number of able women with titles and a higher level of salaries. The faculty already has such women. They should have the salaries and titles."

Mody's convictions about fair recognition extended through all faculty concerns. They also included the whole staff—at one time lumped under the archaic title, "non-academic personnel." On this point he was emphatic: "Yes, I will join any sort of movement to abolish the false and unfair label of 'non-academic personnel' now used to describe the University staff. A great many distinguished faculty members would be less so if it were not for 'non-academics.' Anyway, I like one-word descriptions like 'Staff,' 'Faculty,' 'Administration.' "

Mody was a champion of students; he therefore had a constant interest in teaching. He did not separate instruction from any primary goal of the University. Annually he repeated, in effect, this initial comment on rewards for effective teaching, submitted when he first became chairman: "I have signed all the recommendations for promotion based solely on teaching. Let's not wait until budget councils are unanimous on this policy. Budget councils as they now operate are not going to be unanimous about anything, including classroom work."

Mody's first experience included not only work at a teachers college but also an assignment in a "demonstration school." Asked for his opinion about common interests of education and the liberal arts, he answered:

> I think that the hostility between Arts and Sciences on the one hand and "professional" education on the other is exaggerated. Possibly it exists elsewhere; there is no reason for it at Texas. One of the best UT programs in early years sent full pro-

fessors around the state for interviewing (and I think testing) high school students who wanted to come here. I think senior professors, now gone, did a superb job of this sort of hard work (it certainly wasn't public relations), and I understand that one of our great biologists intends to work with high school students when he retires.

Mody's talents for hard work—especially when his efforts could aid a students or a colleague—were Herculean. They were more remarkable because of the fact that he was less robust than some of those whom he assisted. I remember one doctoral examination that illustrates the point. Mody had been put on the committee at the last minute because of some unexpected emergency. He got a copy of the dissertation the day before the examination. The ceremonial questioning was average for such occasions—some encouraging comments, some careful inquiry, some suggestions about later publication. When it came Mody's time to question the candidate, he handed him about fifty pages of careful notes with the practical comment, "These may make your work more accurate." When the committee adjourned, one of us observed that Mody must have spent more than daylight hours helping that student. As he disappeared out the door, Mody grinned. "Couldn't sleep anyway," he said.

This volume is an appropriate collection of Mody's shorter pieces. It seems likely that the Boatright research on the cowboy may some day become his most widely recognized work. His search for material went on many years. At times the labor must have been a burden, but he never lightened his obligation to get at the whole record. Nor was he distracted by trivial, romantic account. The Boatright Collection, given to the University by his widow and family, will stir future students to continue his work. Besides this collection, Mody assisted the University's acquisition of numerous resources that did not touch his "specialty."

Despite the urging of friends, Mody never wrote a full account of his boyhood. Unlike writers whose autobiographical accounts have ranged from Dickensian pathos to idylls of bright youth, Mody had total and totally realistic recall of his growing up. His recollections, which he seldom worded even to close friends, informed and guided his later years. So in a figurative sense his beginnings are written large in what he became and in much of what he did.

A final word about Mody's letters. During his lifetime, the age of letter-writing is said to have come to an end. Yet Mody was a prolific writer of messages. His official correspondence is noteworthy for two qualities. The first is rare; not one message he ever sent "through channels" was self-serving. The second is somewhat more common; he was concise, but his brevity was full of meaning. For his letter of retirement from the faculty he required only a few lines.

Mody's more personal letters—nearly always handwritten— were mainly notes of encouragement, sympathy, friendly disagreement, or shared pleasure. Those letters are scattered now, perhaps too widely for collection. Over the years, they entered into the lives of those who got them. Like conversations with him and his steadfast friendship, they left reason for gratitude.

That gratitude will outlast the night.

HARRY H. RANSOM
Chancellor Emeritus
The University of Texas System

INTRODUCTION

The rationale for this volume is relatively simple. Mody Boatright's publishing career extended from 1927 until the year of his death, 1970. Over the years his shorter contributions to the literature of folklore and cultural history were highly significant, and, although many of his articles were later to be incorporated into books, several of the books are out of print, and the fugitive pieces are scattered in assorted journals and folklore collections. This anthology, by bringing together his more important and representative pieces, will both show something of the scope of his work and make available the essence of his contribution to American folklore studies.

There are four areas to which Boatright devoted his principal efforts: the cowboy, the American frontier, the oil industry, and folklore and the folklorist in contemporary society. These areas may seem disparate, but they have an essential unity.

First, Boatright was not a compartmentalist; while dealing with the particulars of one facet of his interests he never lost sight of the total picture into which that facet, the other facets, and the other interests fit. He was a cultural historian who happened to approach culture from the angle of folklore, but that approach did not warp his view of society as a whole. His frequent criticisms of the "professional" folklorists, who were too often, he felt, reluctant to study folklore in terms of the total culture, demonstrate both his distaste for any narrowness and his willingness to speak his mind when he felt there was ample cause.

Folk tradition, beliefs, motifs, and attitudes were then for him simply one aspect of the culture complex. And he fully recognized, as any conscious soul today must, that culture changes, but that there are continuing factors even in the midst of that change, many of them in the area of folklore. Boatright was born into one tradition, that of the range cattle industry that grew up in the West in the years just before his birth. But even as he absorbed that culture, he sought to expand his view and his knowledge; he earned a doctorate in English literature in a department that did not see folklore as worthy of the primary interests of a real scholar. He found history an equally broadening discipline in which to expand his knowledge of culture. Thus he built a broad base for his specialization, and he could then look at cultural change and the role of folklore in culture with a wide perspective.

It was only natural that the lore of the cowboy should have been his first interest. Since Lomax and others had already collected most of the cowboy songs by the time he became seriously interested in folklore, his interest turned toward the yarns. The first selection is a collection of Pecos Bill stories, which later appeared in different form in *Tall Tales from Texas Cow Camps*. This first phase of his interest in the cowboy was to expand later to a projected study (virtually complete at his death) of the rise of the cowboy as an American folk hero, whose popularity has been consistently demonstrated from the day of the dime novel to this year's television shows. Two articles meant to be incorporated in that book are included here, "Theodore Roosevelt, Social Darwinism, and the Cowboy" and "The American Myth Rides the Range." They demonstrate Boatright's view of a folk-hero type in the light of contemporary social thought.

Since the cowboy was a figure who rose on the frontier, it was only natural that Boatright should have turned his attention to the frontier as a whole. *Folk Laughter on the American Frontier*, in addition to being a compendium of frontier humor, indicates conclusively that the frontiersman laughed, not out of despair, but out of buoyant good humor ("Frontier Humor: Despairing or Buoyant?"). Because so much of this humor involved tall yarns, there is also a chapter on the tall tale ("The Art of Tall Lying") in which Boatright shows that these tales are produced in accordance with a discernible and demanding folk art form.

Boatright, however, did not see the frontiersman as simply a spinner of yarns. "The Myth of Frontier Individualism" examines frontier life in detail and refutes the then prevailing notion that rugged individualism was an inheritance from the American frontier. While it is not, in one sense, a folklore study, it is a study in folk culture and practice, and it explodes a deliberately fabricated myth. It exemplifies Boatright's broader view of the folk.

The oil industry was expanding over Texas at the time Boatright was himself expanding his consciousness of the world around him. And the oil industry partook of much he was familiar with: it was a new thing with its own pioneers and it had its tale tellers. He saw that here was a new field into which the folk would carry their old traditions to have them change form and bend to meet new circumstances, but in which much would prevail. Two articles, later a part of *Folklore of the Oil Industry*, ("Aunt Cordie's Ax and Other Motifs in Oil" and "The Oil Promoter as Trickster") show the folk manner of dealing with new phenomena in terms of older attitudes.

In his study of Gib Morgan, Boatright delineated the career and tales of the folk hero of a major industry. As a teller of tall tales, Morgan was a practitioner of the folk art form Boatright had cut his teeth on. That he told tales of gigantic derricks

and wells that flowed buttermilk instead of ones about blue
northers and rattlesnake fangs imbedded in boot heels was sec-
ondary; his method was the same. Boatright shows that Morgan
deserves his place in the folk hierarchy of Munchausens ("Gib
Morgan among the Heroes").

His last published book, *Tales from the Derrick Floor*, written
with William A. Owens, is, as its subtitle proclaims, a folk
history of the oil industry, and it contains transcriptions from
the hundreds of tapes Boatright and Owens made of the recollections of pioneers in the industry.

As the frontier faded back into time and after his investiga-
tions of the folk when confronted with a new way of life in the
oil fields, Boatright quite logically began to look at the scene
with a two-pronged view. On the one hand there are the folk
crafts, the particulars of the life of the folk on the frontier and
during the years before industrialization engulfed rural America, and the bits and pieces of lore to be found in the stories of
their past that every family transmits to its succeeding generations. Boatright, in "How Will Boatright Made Bits and Spurs"
and "The Family Saga as a Form of Folklore," suggests that
contemporary collectors record this way of life and these stories
before they are irretrievably lost.

The other prong of his view saw the folklorist as having to
deal in terms of his traditional way of thinking with a society
in which the oral tradition is being replaced by new media and
in which the older concepts of myth are no longer relevant. With
institutions taking on mythological significance and personification, there must be a reevaluation, not in terms of theme, but
in terms of function, of the role of myth. ("On the Nature of
Myth" and "Folklore in a Literate Society.")

Boatright's progression from hearing tall tales from cowhands
on a West Texas ranch in his boyhood to examining contemporary problems in folklore is a logical one. He grew with his
time, and, just as he saw the changing circumstances of the folk,

he saw the need for the folklorist's operating in terms of that change.

Boatright was then both collector and interpreter of folklore, but never mere classifier, for he saw the role and duty of the folklorist as that of the historian of the folk, who are, of course, members of a society in the light of which they must be seen. Folklore was for him a basic expression of human belief, feeling, and practice, and the study of so important a segment of human life from Boatright's vantage point could not fail to produce an important contribution to the study of American folklore and of American life.

ERNEST B. SPECK
Sul Ross State University
Alpine, Texas

ACKNOWLEDGMENTS

I wish to acknowledge with gratitude the permissions granted by the following for the use of material reprinted in this volume:

Journal of American Folklore for "How Will Boatright Made Bits and Spurs," copyright © 1970 by the American Folklore Society.

Social Science Quarterly for "The Myth of Frontier Individualism," copyright © 1941 by the Southwestern Social Science Association.

Southwest Review for "The Genius of Pecos Bill," copyright © 1929 by Mody C. Boatright; "Frontier Humor: Despairing or Buoyant?" copyright © 1941, 1969 by Mody C. Boatright and reprinted by permission of The Macmillan Company; "The Art of Tall Lying," copyright © 1969 by Mody C. Boatright and reprinted by permission of The Macmillan Company; "The American Myth Rides the Range: Owen Wister's Man on Horseback," copyright © 1951 by Mody C. Boatright; "On the Nature of Myth," copyright © 1954 by Southern Methodist University Press.

The Texas Folklore Society for "Gib Morgan among the Heroes," copyright © 1945 by Mody C. Boatright, copyright renewed 1973 by Mrs. Mody C. Boatright; "Aunt Cordie's Ax and Other Motifs in Oil," copyright © 1953 by the Texas Folklore

Society; "Folklore in a Literate Society," copyright © 1958 by the Texas Folklore Society; "The Oil Promoter as Trickster," copyright © 1969 by the Texas Folklore Society.

The Texas Quarterly for "Theodore Roosevelt, Social Darwinism, and the Cowboy," copyright © 1964 by The University of Texas at Austin.

The University of Illinois Press for "The Family Saga as a Form of Folklore," copyright © 1958 by the Board of Trustees of the University of Illinois.

Mrs. Mody C. Boatright on behalf of the Boatright estate.

E. B. S.

Mody Boatright, Folklorist

A COLLECTION OF ESSAYS

1. The Genius of Pecos Bill
(1929)

MUCH has been written of the open range and of the large ranch which succeeded it. The mores of the cowboy have been discussed with varying degrees of accuracy. His ballads have been before the public for a number of years. So thoroughly have John A. Lomax, J. Frank Dobie, and others combed this field that we may now rest assured that all of the cowboy songs of any considerable distribution have been printed.

This is not true, however, of another large body of literature coming from the open range and the cattle ranch. The cowboy sang at night to soothe his cattle; he sang during the day to keep them in motion. He created fiction for an entirely different purpose.

While it is true that the cowboy deserves his reputation for

NOTE: Originally published in *Southwest Review* 14 (July 1929): 418–428.

reticence, it is also true that when conditions were favorable for the exercise of his art, he was an inveterate liar who took an intense delight in "loading" the greenhorn. This pastime, which usually occupied the hours in the evening after supper, consisted in telling "windies" for the benefit of the tenderfoot or the tourist. If the auditor seemed the least bit credulous, the narrators went on vying with each other, heaping exaggeration upon exaggeration. Sometimes the listener was informed by a sell at the end of the story that he had been taken in; more often he was made aware of the fact by the sheer heights of impossibility to which the narrative ascended; occasionally he accepted the story in good faith and went away neither sadder nor wiser.

Real or mythological animals, reptiles, insects, strange weather phenomena, feats of horsemanship and marksmanship, and adventures of various sorts furnished the materials of cowboy fiction. The cowboy did not scruple to make use of whatever he may have heard, sometimes adapting Münchhausen to local conditions with surprising ingenuity. The result was a literature at once imaginative, robust, and humorous: one in striking contrast to the pensive and melancholy ballads, which taken in themselves present a one-sided picture of the cowboy's character.

The cowboy's hero was in no strict sense a supernatural character: he merely possessed to the highest degree endurance, agility, and other qualities which the cowboy of necessity exemplified, and which he consequently admired. The hero of cowboy fiction could drink his coffee boiling hot and wipe his mouth on a prickly-pear; but unlike Paul Bunyan, he was not a giant, the impact of whose body in being thrown from a horse or a tornado could form the Great Basin of the West.

Nor did cowboy fiction ever become unified around a single character. When a hero was needed, his name might be invented on the spot; the feats of daring might be ascribed to some local character; or the narrator himself might appropriate the honors.

Unification, however, seems to have been under weigh; and had not industrial progress put an end to the heroic age in the Southwest, likely Pecos Bill would have supplanted his rivals and become the Paul Bunyan of the Southwest.

II

What the name of Pecos Bill's daddy was nobody professes to know. In his day it was a trifle impolite, not to say indiscreet, to ask one how he was called back in the States. More than one tenderfoot, ignorant of this nicety of etiquette, perished at the muzzle of a smoking gun. If the stranger did not signify how he was to be called, those familiar with the ways of the land bestowed upon him the most likely cognomen that the imagination could on the spur of the moment conjure up. Pecos Bill's daddy was therefore called the Ole Man, first, because he was old— about seventy-five when he came to Texas—and, secondly, because that was the only epithet his wife ever used in addressing him. For similar reasons she was called the Ole Woman.

About the time Davy Crockett told Tennessee to go to hell, the Ole Man and the Ole Woman loaded their twelve kids and their personal and household effects, consisting of a squirrel rifle, a chopping-axe, and an iron hog-rendering kettle, on the wagon, yoked in Spot and Buck, and started for Texas. Having marked the trail for their successors with dead Indians, they reached the Sabine River, and there they halted. The Ole Man gathered his issue about him and made them a speech. It was brief and to the point, as the Ole Man's utterances usually were. He said: "On the other side is Texas, wild and woolly and full of fleas. If ye ain't that a-way only more so, ye ain't no offspring of mine."

They then forded the river and camped for the night; and that night Pecos Bill was born. The next morning the Ole Woman put him on a bear-skin and left him to amuse himself while she made the corn-pone for breakfast.

Suddenly it got dark. The Ole Man and the Ole Woman at first did not know what to make of this strange phenomenon, but soon they heard music. They had heard sounds faintly resembling these before. Mosquitoes! They looked to their infant. They could not see him. He was completely enveloped in a swarm of mosquitoes. The Ole Man felt his way to the wagon and got out his rifle. He thought he might be able to scare the mosquitoes away by firing into the air. He pointed the muzzle of the gun toward the sky and pulled the trigger. A faint ray of light came through. It was as though you were looking at the sky through a small tube from a dark room. But the hole soon closed up, and it looked as though Pecos Bill would at any moment be carried off.

Then another idea came to the Ole Man. He groped his way to the wagon and brought out the hog-rendering kettle. He fought the mosquitoes back, turned this over Pecos Bill, and slipped the chopping axe under the edge for the chap to play with. The mosquitoes buzzed and buzzed around the kettle. Presently one backed off, the others opening a way for him, and came at that kettle like a bat shot out of a cannon. He hit the kettle and rammed his bill clean through it; and he stuck. Then another one backed off and came at the kettle; and he stuck. Then they kept backing off and coming at the kettle, and every one stuck. The Ole Man and the Ole Woman stood watching the mosquitoes ram the kettle. After each insect (varmints, they should have been called) struck the kettle, a metallic ring was audible. Pretty soon the Ole Man and Ole Woman got on to what was happening. Every time a bill would come through, Pecos would brad it with the chopping axe. After a while those mosquitoes just naturally lifted the kettle and flew off with it. The others thought they had Pecos Bill and followed the kettle away. Of course the Ole Man hated to lose the kettle. He said he didn't know how the Ole Woman was going to render up the lard and bear's grease; but it was worth a hundred kettles, he said, to know that he had such a smart brat. And from that day he began to speak of Bill as a chap of Great Possibilities. He felt sure that with the proper raising he would make a great man, and he began giving him a diet of jerked game with whiskey and onions for breakfast.

The Ole Man first settled on a sandy hill on the Trinity River somewhere east of where Dallas now is. It happened in this way. They were traveling west in their customary manner, the Ole Man and the six oldest kids walking alongside Spot and Buck, and the Ole Woman and the seven youngest kids in the wagon. Just as they were reaching the foot of a sandy hill, a heavy rain came up. It rained so hard that the Ole Man couldn't see the wagon, but by keeping close to his trusty oxen, he managed to drive them up the hill. By the time he got to the top, it had quit raining. He looked back and saw the wagon still at the foot of the hill, with the kids that had been walking with him under it. He was using a rawhide lariat for a log-chain, and it had got wet and stretched, so that, though he had driven the oxen nearly a mile up the slope, he had not moved the wagon an inch.

The sun got brighter and brighter, and while the Ole Man was wondering what to do next, Ole Spot dropped dead of sunstroke.

"Worth his weight in gold, that brute," sighed the Ole Man. "Recken I might as well skin him."

While the Ole Man was skinning Spot, a norther came up and Buck keeled over, frozen to death.

"Well, Ole Woman, bring up the brats," shouted the Ole Man. "I recken we might as well stop here," he added philosophically, wiping a tear from his eye with the handle of his Bowie knife.

He threw the yoke over a stump. The wife and the kids brought up the bedding and some chuck from the wagon. After they had eaten supper and the kids were tucked in bed, the Ole Man tried to blow out the lantern, which he had lighted during the meal, but it would not blow. He found it frozen stiff and cold as an icicle. He broke it off and buried it in the sand.

The next morning was clear and warm and sunshiny. While the family was eating breakfast, the Ole Man looked down and saw the wagon coming right up the hill. The rawhide was drying out. When the wagon reached the brow of the hill, the Ole Man got out the chopping axe and began felling logs for his cabin.

At first the Ole Man was badly handicapped on account of the loss of his oxen, for while game was plentiful, the Ole Man never felt that he had eaten unless he had had corn-pone or yams, or both. Then, too, his supply of corn whiskey was getting low. He just had to have a corn patch. He soon discovered that the Ole Woman and the kids could pull the Georgia-stock he had improvised out of wood. He put in a patch, and soon was living a peaceful life, killing Indians and game, and growing corn and yams.

Usually when the other members of the family were in the field, Bill would be left alone in the cabin. One day just as the Ole Man had turned the Ole Woman and the kid he had hitched up with her around to start on another row, the Ole Woman happened to glance toward the cabin. She began trying to get out of the harness, yelling to the Ole Man that she had seen a panther go into the cabin where Bill had been left alone. (Bill was now about three years old.)

The Ole Man told her not to get excited, that it was a half-hour by sun till dinner time yet. The dang panther, he said, needn't expect any help from him. The fool critter ought to have had more sense than to go in there where Bill was.

So they ploughed till noon, and when they came back to the cabin, they found Bill chewing on a piece of raw panther flank.

This peaceful life went on for another year or so, but came a time when the even tenor of the Ole Man's way was rudely disturbed. One day when the Ole Man had the Ole Woman and one of the kids hitched to the Georgia-stock, a piece of paper came blowing across the field. The Ole Woman and the kid went

rearing and tearing across the field, dragging the Ole Man after
them. They finally got loose and tore up the Georgia-stock. Then
after a while they quieted down, and the Ole Man picked up the
piece of paper where it had caught on a stump. It was an old
newspaper.

The next morning he began to investigate. He found wagon
tracks within five miles of his place. He followed them for fifty
miles up the river and there he found a new cabin. He came
home and told the Ole Woman and the kids to get ready to
leave. The country, he said, was getting too thickly settled for
him. He and the kids went out and ran down a couple of mustangs. He hitched them to the wagon with some harness he had
made from the hides of Spot and Buck, loaded up his family and
his property, and headed west.

To tell how Pecos Bill was lost by the Ole Man on the banks of
the Pecos River, how he grew up with the coyotes, how he all
but exterminated the vicious godaphroes, how he invented ways
of capturing the sly whiffle-pooffle and the shyer milamo bird; to
relate his adventures as buffalo hunter, cattleman, railroad con-
tractor, and to detail his many other exploits would require a
volume. These things, interesting as they are, I must omit; and
having given an authentic account of the genesis of the great
hero, I now pass to his exodus.

III

Pecos Bill has gone the way of the open range and the Texas
longhorn. On that point all the old cattlemen are agreed. But just
how and when and where the great hero passed in his checks is
apparently to remain unknown. Most of the witnesses to the
deeds herein chronicled have died; some live on to testify from
memories made dim by senility; and of these latter, some few,
alas, are downright liars. But without exception, each is ready to
defend with his life his pet theory of how Pecos Bill met his

death, and not a few have died with their boots on in just that way.

At one time there was in Texas one Gabriel Asbury Jackson. Having worked himself out of a job in Kansas, this gentleman came to Texas to buck the cigarette evil. Once in Amarillo he cornered a group of young cowpunchers who were too drunk to make a getaway and addressed them somewhat as follows:

"Young gentlemen, beware of the cigarette. You think you are smart to smoke a sack of Bull Durham a day, do you? Well, look at Pecos Bill. A stalwart young man he was, tough as nails, a fine specimen. But he got to fooling with cigarettes. What did they do for him? Nothing at first. He smoked on with impunity. He puffed away for ninety years, but finally they got him. And they'll get you, every mother's son, if you don't leave them alone."

Gabriel Jackson's theory, however, is given little credence by the old cattlemen of the Southwest. Indeed, it is reported that one old trail-driver, who happened by just in time to hear the dramatic appeal quoted above, was so incensed that he made the speaker eat his words at the point of a six-shooter, and thus disproved for all time this spurious account of the hero's death.

Bill, however, was an incessant smoker, though he did not smoke Bull Durham. He concocted a smoking mixture of his own invention, the chief ingredients being Kentucky homespun, sulphur, and gun powder. When matches were scarce, Bill used to ride out into a thunder-storm and light his cigarette with a streak of lightning. This practice doubtless led to another story of Bill's death that has had considerable circulation: namely, that he was struck by lightning. But none of the old-timers who saw Bill, on a bet, throw a surcingle over a streak of lightning and ride it over Pike's Peak will ever believe that story.

A good many of them do accept the theory that it was liquor that killed poor Bill. Brought up as he was from tender youth on a diet of whiskey and onions, Bill was still a young **man** when whiskey lost all of its kick for him. He got to putting nitro-glycerin in his toddies. This worked for a while; but soon he had to go to wolf-bait, and from that to fish-hooks. Bill used to say, rather sorrow-like, that that was the only way he could get an idea from his booze. But the fish-hooks after about fifty years rusted out his interior, and brought poor Bill to an early grave. Some of Bill's contemporaries maintain, with some plausibility, that this account is just a damn lie concocted by the prohibition men.

A few of these dissenters will tell you exactly how Bill met his death. They say that once in Fort Worth he met a Boston man with a mail-order cowboy outfit on. When Bill saw him, he just naturally lay down and laughed himself to death. Others attempt to refute this story by pointing out the fact that the burial records of Fort Worth contain no mention of Pecos Bill.

Perhaps the following story is nearer than any other to the truth. It is claimed by some that Pecos Bill drifted into Cheyenne just as the first rodeo was being held. Being a bit curious to know what it was all about, Bill went out to the grounds and looked over the riders and the ropers; then he began to weep. Finally when a country lawyer, just three years out of Mississip-pi, got up to make a speech and referred to the men on horseback as cowboys, Bill turned white and began to tremble; and when the country lawyer went on to speak of keeping "inviolate the sacred traditions of the Old West," Bill went out and crawled in a prairie-dog hole and died of solemncholy.

After several years, when all of Bill's would-be rivals were confident that he was dead, they began to try to defame his character. Their man charge was that he was a hot-headed, over-bearing sort of fellow: in short, though few dared use the word, that he was a "killer."

Now Pecos Bill did kill lots of men—he himself lost count long before he died—but he never killed for profit, and he seldom killed a man without just cause. His enemies talked up his shoot-

ing of Big Ike for snoring. But they would always leave out the
most important part of the story. They would not mention the
fact that Bill had been standing guard every night for six weeks
and was beginning to get a bit sleepy. They would not mention,
either, the fact that the outfit was in Indian country, and every
old trail-driver knows what a snorer in camp during Indian
trouble means.

Then there was Ris Risbone. Ris was a practical joker who
ramrodded an outfit that fell in behind Bill's on the trail. Ris had
a great store of jokes, some dozen in all, and when he pulled one,
he slapped his knees and laughed and laughed. One day Ris rode
up to Bill's chuck wagon when there was nobody in sight but
the cook, and he was asleep in the shade of the wagon with his
head between the wheels. Ris slipped up and grabbed the trace
chains and began shaking them, yelling, "Whoa! Whoa!" The
poor cook woke up thinking that the team was running away and
that he was about to get his pass to Saint Peter. He jumped up
and bumped his head on the wagon, then looked around and saw
Ris standing there slapping his knees and laughing. Just then Bill
rode up. He didn't say anything.

When the outfits got to Abilene, Bill paid off his men, and
they all went into the White Elephant to take a drink. Just as
Bill was about to drop the fish-hooks into his glass, Ris poked his
head in at the window and yelled "Fire! Fire!"—and Bill did.

In one killing, however, Bill acted a bit hasty, as he himself
afterwards admitted. One day he called Three-fingered Hank
out of the saloon, saying that he wanted to speak to him in private. Bill led Hank out into a back alley, and there they stopped.

"Say, Hank," asked Bill, looking him in the eye, "didn't you
say that Red Mike said that I was a hot-headed, overbearing sort
of man?"

"Naw," says Hank, "Yer mistook me. He never said that."

"Well, doggone," says Bill; "ain't that too bad. I've gone and
killed an innocent man."

2. The Myth of Frontier Individualism (1941)

There is no more persistent myth in American history than the myth that rugged individualism is or has been the way of American life. Many influences have entered into the creation of this myth, but the man who is chiefly responsible for its general acceptance is Frederick Jackson Turner, who, in 1893, when the western states were loud in their demands for national regulation of industry, said in his now famous Chicago address that the American frontier had promoted democracy—a democracy "strong in selfishness and individualism, intolerant of experience and education, and pressing individual liberty beyond its proper bounds." Its tendency, he said, was antisocial. "It produced antipathy to control, and particularly to any direct control." It

NOTE: Originally published in *Southwestern Social Science Quarterly* 22 (July 1941): 12–32.

permitted "lax business honor, inflated paper currency and wild-cat banking."[1]

Later industrialists, harassed by popular western agitation for social control of industry, seized upon Turner's pronouncement as a justification of their Manchester economics. For had he not said that the frontier had been the dominant force in the shaping of American ideals and that the way of the frontier was uncontrolled individual initiative? E. H. Harriman, alarmed by governmental concern over the financing and operation of his railroads, issued a statement calculated to convince the western agrarians that such regulation as was being attempted by the Interstate Commerce Commission was a violation of our early pioneer ideals. Herbert Hoover took up the cry in 1922 and has since continued to denounce "regimentation" and to proclaim his gospel of "rugged individualism" of which he finds the "American frontier the epic expression."[2] James Truslow Adams and others swell the chorus.

Although liberals and radicals, whose socioeconomic philosophy differs from that of the United States Chamber of Commerce and the National Manufacturers' Association, have pointed out that our national industrial policy has been one of paternalism rather than of individualism, they have for the most part accepted or questioned only timidly the Turner-Hoover interpretation of frontier democracy. Ernest Boyd's statement is typical: "Yesterday all the slogans and catchwords that beguile them [the apostles of rugged individualism] were true."[3] Parrington thought it odd that it was in the West that the spirit of social protest should "first express itself most adequate-

[1] Frederick Jackson Turner, *The Significance of the Frontier in American History* (New York, 1920), pp. 30ff.

[2] Herbert Hoover, "American Individualism," *World's Work* 43: 585.

[3] Ernest Boyd, "Drugged Individualism," *American Mercury* 33:308–314.

ly."[4] Charles Beard, who several years ago announced that "our fundamental philosophy of rugged individualism must be modified to meet the needs of a cooperative age,"[5] has more recently expressed the opinion that Turner "overworked the 'individualism' of the frontier,"[6] but his protest is tentative and overcautious. Henry Wallace speaks of "frontier freebooter democracy of the purely individualistic type."[7]

That there were freebooters on the frontier no one can deny; for the frontier attracted freebooters as a dead steer attracts buzzards. They came from the Atlantic seaboard, and they came also from England and Scotland and Germany. Some of them, though not as many as Turner implies, grew up in a frontier environment; but that they were products of frontier ideology can be demonstrated only when it can be demonstrated that all freebooters of whatever age, climate, or nationality are the products of a frontier ideology. If the liberals would read the documents of frontier history, and particularly the memoirs of frontiersmen, they would find many facts which have been ignored or underemphasized by the Turner school of historians, but which call for a modification of the dominant conception of the frontier environment. They would not find the frontier the Hobbesian state of nature our mythology has made it. They would no longer confuse governmental policies determined by an Eastern governing class with the social philosophy of the Western folk. They would learn to distinguish between the conspicuous individuals who exploited the frontier (and the frontiersmen) on a grand scale and the people who settled in the West seeking a fuller life than had been their lot elsewhere.

[4] Vernon Louis Parrington, *Main Currents of American Thought* (New York, 1930), vol. 3, p. 319.

[5] Charles A Beard, "The Myth of Rugged Individualism," *Harper's Magazine* 164:13–22.

[6] *New Republic* 97:359–362.

[7] Henry A. Wallace, *New Frontiers* (New York, 1934), p. 277.

One who examines the folkways of the settlers is impressed by the numerous ways in which the principle of mutuality finds expression in frontier life.

First of all, it is manifest in the pattern of Western settlement, a pattern early established and repeated many times with variations. The land policies of the colonies and later of the United States were shaped by men to whose interest it was to keep wages low and land values high. They did not wish to encourage emigration. Rather, they were in constant fear that their labor supply would be drained off by the West. Land acts, therefore, favored the industrialist, the seaboard farmer, and the land speculator. Even after the Republican party had won the 1860 election by trading homesteads for votes, the homesteads provided were throughout the greater part of the West inadequate for the support of a family; no provision was made for getting the needy settler to the land; and no paternalistic legislation protected his infant industry when he got there. Hence it may be said, as the Beards have said, that the people who went west went as individuals.[8] But this is not to say that they went singly. Traders and trappers and hunters might venture into the wilderness or onto the plains in parties of a half-dozen or so; but those who went expecting to occupy the Indians' land went in larger groups. In the absence of any governmental provision for group migration, they usually went under the leadership of some promoter of a scheme of colonization. This promoter might be a land speculator like Robertson or his agent Boone; he might be a religious leader like Young; he might be a philanthropist like Prince Carl Solms-Braunfels, who brought hundreds of Germans to Texas; he might (under Spanish law) be a legally constituted impresario like Austin. He was, in the later phase of settlement, often the agent of a railroad.

[8] Charles A. and Mary R. Beard, *The Rise of American Civilization* (New York, 1930), vol. 1, p. 509.

When a sufficient number of families had been enlisted to give some assurance of protection against the Indians at the place of settlement, the migration began. If an overland journey was involved, the travelers organized under strict discipline for mutual protection. Upon arriving at their destination, they erected a community blockhouse, or other fortification, where in times of danger they could "fort up." From these earlier nuclei other communities branched out and other forts were erected. The duty of informal military service devolved upon all able-bodied men. Their common danger and their common poverty promoted a strong corporate life.

Perhaps J. B. Finley had forgotten some of the local quarrels when he wrote of the settlers in the Ohio Valley at the beginning of the nineteenth century: "There was never a healthier, happier, more hospitable or cheerful people. Their interests were one, and their dependence upon each other was indispensable, and all things were in common. Thus united, they lived as one family."[9] But there is abundant evidence of the correctness of his essential description. Noah Smithwick, Texas frontiersman, wrote:

> Our common danger was a strong tie to bind us together. No matter what our personal feelings were, when in response to the sound of galloping hoofs, in the middle of the night, which we all knew heralded a tale of blood, we started from our beds and were at the door in anticipation of the "hello" which prefaced a harrowing story of a neighbor slain and his family either sharing his fate, or worse still, carried away into horrible captivity, we hastily saddled our horses, if the Indians had not been ahead of us, and left our wives and children, to avenge the atrocious deed.[10]

After the danger of Indian raids was over, the pattern of set-

[9] J. B. Finley, *Autobiography* (Cincinnati, 1853), pp. 70–71.
[10] Noah Smithwick, *The Evolution of a State* (Austin, 1910), pp. 239–240.

tlement was not materially altered. Group migration was even more conspicuous, partly because greater numbers of people were willing to migrate. Whole church congregations, sometimes virtually whole communities where shifting economic conditions brought hard times, came to the plains of Nebraska and Kansas and other western states, not infrequently under the protection of some organization like the New England Emigrant Aid Society. They came to found communities where they could enjoy a corporate life, typically not with the aim of establishing communistic societies but of re-creating on the frontier the simple agrarian and handicraft economy that industrialism was soon to destroy.

They erected their homes, their schools, and their churches by cooperative labor. The logrolling and the house-raising became characteristic frontier institutions. They helped each other plow and harvest. The cattle roundup began as a cooperative cowhunt in the mountains of the South; it maintained its cooperative character until the range was all fenced; and it is still cooperative among all but the largest ranchers. The reminiscences of the trail drivers of Texas stress mutual help, not individualism.

In 1863 [writes P. D. Butler] came the great drouth. The Nueces and San Antonio Rivers became mere trickling threads of water with here and there a small pool. The grass was soon gone and no cattle survived except those that had previously drifted across the Nueces River on to a range that was not so severely affected by the drouth. In 1864 rains came and plentiful grass, and a search for drifted cattle was organized. All the young, able-bodied men were in the army, so a party of forty-five boys and old men, headed by Uncle Billy Ricks, of Oakville, went to San Diego to the ranch of Benito Lopez, from which point they worked for a month rounding up cattle and cutting out those of their own brands. Every week a herd was taken across the river and headed for home, and in this way

500 head were put back on the ranges of Karnes County, where thousands had grazed before the drouth.[11]

If a widow had no men in her family, her cattle would be gathered and her calves branded with her own brand. If a neighbor were sick, his corn would be plowed for him. If his house burnt down, neighbors contributed food and labor and clothing. If a school or church was to be built, each contributed his share of materials and labor. Not all pioneers have put into their memoirs the piety of John Carr of Middle Tennessee, but the incident he relates is typical of hundreds:

> We determined to build us a house to worship the God of our fathers in. We had a meeting, purchased a piece of ground on a beautiful eminence, convenient to a fine spring. We appointed a day to get timbers to build our house. When the day arrived, it was wonderful to behold the multitude of people that came out—wagons and teams, choppers and hewers. There could not have been less than forty or fifty men on the ground. By evening we had laid the foundation; and it was proposed we should have prayer before we parted. . . . When we arose from our knees, I was requested to name the house. I saw such a spirit of brotherly love and union . . . I told them we would call it Union.[12]

Frontier hospitality, commented upon by practically every traveling writer who reached the frontier, was not due solely, as some of these travelers have egotistically imagined, to the settler's loneliness and hunger for news of the outside world. It grew rather out of the relationship of men engaged in a common struggle with distance and heat and drouth and blizzards and grasshoppers.

Such activities as these are evidence of a strong corporate feel-

---

[11] Marvin Hunter, ed., *Trail Drivers of Texas* (Nashville, 1925), p. 481.
[12] John Carr, *Early Times in Middle Tennessee* (Nashville, 1867), pp. 154–155.

ing whereby the individual found deep satisfaction in identifying himself with the group. It would be a mistake, however, to infer that when the pioneer contributed to the recreational life of the community, donated a beef for the barbecue, shared his food with a traveler, helped his neighbor round up and brand his cattle, or plowed his sick neighbor's corn, he was indulging in mere philanthropy. His hospitality and his generous welcome to newcomers might have had some relation to land values. He helped his neighbor with his cattle because he needed his neighbor's help. He nursed his sick neighbor because he himself might need nursing. It wasn't that he expected immediate or specific repayment in kind. It was that he wanted the feeling of security that came from knowing that his fellows would bolster him so that stringent emergency need not mean permanent disaster. This sort of neighborly cooperation was the frontier's answer to the problem of social security.

Now cooperation involves some degree of social control, and Osgood and Turner and others who have made the pioneer impatient of control *per se* have misinterpreted him. He resented regimentation by the governing class in the East, but he did not hesitate to regiment himself, and, in so far as he was able, others whose interests conflicted with his.

This regimentation came about, in the first place, by the development of a set of folkways, a body of American common law, which no Blackstone has ever codified, and which was usually enforced only by public opinion, although frontier magistrates like David Crockett who were ignorant of the law books and who gave their decisions not on "law learning," but on "the principles of common justice and honesty between man and man and . . . natural born sense,"[13] might proclaim it from the bench. On the plains "it was an unwritten law that upon the outbreak of a [prairie] fire every able-bodied man should come with fire-fight-

[13] *The Autobiography of David Crockett* (New York, 1923), p. 90.

ing equipment. . . . The man who slept while his neighbors fought fire all night was considered a traitor."[14]

> There was an unwritten law, recognized by the good women of the towns as well as of the country, that whenever a party of cowhunters rode up and asked to have bread baked, it mattered not the time of day, the request was to be cheerfully complied with. Not from fear of insult in case of refusal, for each and every cowboy was the champion and defender of womanhood and would have scorned to have uttered a disrespectful word in her presence—but from an accommodating spirit and kindness which was universally characteristic in those frontier days. . . . The sack [of flour] was lifted from the pack horse and brought in, and in due time the bread wallets were once more filled with freshly cooked biscuits, and the cowboys rode away with grateful appreciation.[15]

It should be clear that if the "unwritten law" so often referred to in the memoirs of the frontiersmen seemed to give the individual wide liberty in the defense of his property and his life, it also put definite restrictions upon his use of his property. Acts that would have been regarded as trespass under the British common law and the statutory law of densely settled regions were made legal by the customs of the frontier. For instance, a bona fide traveler could kill game along his route of travel, and the indigenous common law, afterwards enacted by the legislatures of some states, protected him from prosecution by the landowner. He could enter a house in the absence of the owner, and so long as he took only food required for his needs, no frontier court would convict him. He might use the kitchen, but he was expected to leave the dishes clean.

Characteristic of frontier culture were numerous mutual protective associations, many of them extralegal in character.

---

[14] Everett Dick, *The Sod House Frontier* (New York, 1938), p. 219.
[15] *Trail Drivers of Texas*, pp. 196–197.

When the police power broke down, the settlers banded themselves together to establish, if not law, at least order.

At one stage of frontier history the settlers were menaced by well-organized rings of horse thieves, operating by methods subsequently adopted by rings of automobile thieves. The settlers' response was the organization of Anti-Horse-Thief Associations. Such an association was organized at Nemaha, Nebraska, in 1858.[16] Officers were elected, dues were fixed, and "riders" were employed to recover stolen horses and to apprehend thieves. Richard Garland belonged to a similar organization in Iowa. He nailed to his barn door a poster "which proclaimed in bold black letters a warning and a threat, signed by 'the Committee.' " This associaton employed an agent, Jim McCarty, and "its effectiveness," says Hamlin Garland, "was largely due to his swift and fearless action."[17] Garland does not say what happened to the thieves that McCarty apprehended. The usual frontier practice in more settled communities was to turn them over to the courts, but wherever orderly government was interrupted, as it was in Kansas and Nebraska during the fifties and throughout the Southwest during Reconstruction, action was more direct. A mass meeting would be called, a "jury" impaneled, and counsel appointed for the accused. If he was found guilty, he would probably be hanged the same day. Mass executions were not uncommon. A former member of the Oklahoma Anti-Horse-Thief Association remembers the simultaneous hanging of five men to the same tree. This deliberate and considered mass justice is not to be confused with mob violence. It is yet to be proved that it erred more frequently than the courts presided over by learned justices in robes.

The discovery of gold in California in 1848 created a situation unique in history. The miners found themselves in the presence of great wealth in the form of placer gold where there was no

[16] Dick, *The Sod House Frontier* pp. 135–136.
[17] Hamlin Garland, *A Son of the Middle Border* (New York, 1917), p. 146.

law to govern the acquisition of this wealth. Throughout the mining region the Argonauts, although for the most part interested only in getting rich quickly and returning home, exhibited a surprising degree of cooperation. The rights of the group were everywhere made superior to the rights of the individual. The gold, in fact belonging to the United States government and therefore legally subject to the disposal of Congress, was assumed to belong equally to all who could gain access to it, Rules were passed in each camp limiting the size of the claim a man might hold, making the holding of the claim contingent upon use, providing for the numbering and registration of claims, and prescribing the procedure by which a claim might be transferred from one man to another. Disputes were settled by the camps or by committees appointed for the purpose. When Captain Marryat felt that his claim of a hundred square feet was being encroached upon, he appealed to the camp. A committee was appointed which measured the claims and found for Marryat. The trespasser was told "to confine himself to his own territory, which he did."[18]

The miners' reminiscences are practically unanimous concerning the absence of disorder during the first stage of mining. Later, however, the presence of great quantities of portable and unidentifiable wealth attracted criminals from all parts of the United States as well as from Australia and Chile. These were at first summarily dealt with by miners' courts; when they became numerous enough to intimidate an entire camp, or where they seized the local government, as they did at one time in Virginia City, the vigilance committee was the miners' answer.

Another typical frontier development was the claim club, organized to accomplish what the politicians had refused to do: namely, to make the western lands available to needy settlers.

[18] Charles Howard Shinn, *Mining Camps* (New York, 1885), p. 154. Shinn's work is especially valuable because of its copious quotation from primary sources.

These clubs were noted and commented upon by the British traveler Charles Wentworth Dilke, who came to the West in the late 1860s:

> When a new State began to be "settled up"—that is, its lands entered upon by actual settlers, not land-sharks—the inhabitants often found themselves in the wilderness, far in advance of attorneys, courts, and judges. It was their custom when this occurred to divide the territory into districts of fifteen or twenty miles square, and form in each a "claim club" to protect the land-claims, or property of the members. Whenever a question of title arose, a judge and a jury were chosen from among the members to hear and determine the case. The occupancy title was invariably protected up to a certain number of acres, which was differently fixed by different clubs. . . . The United States "Homestead" and "Preemption" laws were founded on the practice of these clubs. The claim clubs interfered only for the protection of their members, but they never scrupled to hang willful offenders against their rules, whether members or outsiders.[19]

Judgments, says Dilke, were usually enforced by the local sheriff. In Kansas, for example, a certain man squatted on a piece of land and sold his preemption claim. He later returned and preempted it under the homestead act and attempted to eject the purchaser. The club took action and directed the sheriff to "put the man away." He was never seen again. The attempted fraud was within the bounds of legality, but clubs did not hesitate to place equity above law. The territorial legislatures of Kansas and Nebraska passed acts allowing the settlers 320 acres of land in spite of the 160-acre limit of the federal statute, and the claim clubs attempted to enforce the territorial laws. In this they were only temporarily successful, as they were also in their efforts to maintain their claims against the railroads.

[19] Charles Wentworth Dilke, *Greater Britain* (London, 1869), vol. 1, pp. 201–202.

Many millions of acres granted by Congress to the railroads were occupied by "squatters"; that is, settlers who because of poverty or negligence had failed to file the papers necessary to give their claims legal validity. When the railroads or the purchasers from the railroads attempted to take possession of the land, they found themselves confronted by a group of organized settlers, who believed, as did the miners of the Sierras, the land titles should be contingent upon occupancy and use. In Kansas the Settlers' Protective Association collected annual dues, employed legal counsel, and kept the cases in litigation for several years. Of course, they eventually lost.[20]

Settlers in the prairie states also organized against the cattlemen. In Sherman County, Kansas, members of such an organization took the following oath: "I do solemnly swear not to tell anything that may lead owners of cattle which are running at large contrary to law and destroying settlers' crops to discover who has killed or crippled or in any way injured these same cattle. . . ."[21] In Montana a jury before deciding the fate of a man charged with killing cattle wished to know whether or not the accused had appropriated the carcasses. In the minds of these jurymen to kill stock for profit was a crime; to kill to protect a land claim was blameless.

These extralegal organizations and their frequently illegal methods by no means prove that the frontier settlers were unfit to live in organized society. They reveal, rather, an attempt to organize a society in which human needs would be superior to special privilege. They reveal the inadequacy of the land laws passed by a Congress subservient to the interests of the industrialists and the land speculators. They show how the settlers by collective action attempted to secure for the needy, i.e., them-

[20] Dick, *The Sod House Frontier*, pp. 353–354.
[21] Ibid., pp. 150ff. See also Ernest Staples Osgood, *The Day of the Cattleman* (Minneapolis, 1927).

selves, a meager share of the public domain which was being so generously handed over to the corporations.

The history of the range cattle industry in the United States exhibits many conflicts resulting from the inadequacy of national legislation; but at no stage of the industry did the cattlemen reveal an incapacity for collective action. In Texas, where the range industry originated, Spanish regulatory law and custom were accepted and modified from time to time as conditions changed. The constitution of the Republic of Texas, following Spanish precedent, declared that all grown unbranded cattle (of which there were thousands) grazing on the public domain were the property of the state. They were *ferae naturae*, ownership to which could be established by capture and branding with a legally registered brand. The ownership of calves was established by the brand of their mothers. Except on the Mexican border, where animosities growing out of the Revolution were strong and where international stealing went on intermittently until suppressed by the Texas Rangers in the 1870s, the development of the range industry was orderly and cooperative until the middle of the Civil War. Up to this time, said Charles Goodnight, it was "an unwritten law to mark and brand every calf in your range to its owner, if you knew him. If the mother cows were strays, or unknown, you branded the calves in the same brand that the cow wore."[22] When, however, practically the entire manpower of the range was in the Confederate Army, "certain men scattered over the country," many of them deserters and draft evaders, began branding for themselves the neglected cattle of the men in service. A loose protective association was formed in Parker County, then on the frontier, but the elderly men and boys were unable to enforce the folkways of the range, and stealing was not suppressed until the restoration of orderly government at the close of the war.

22 J. Evetts Haley, *Charles Goodnight* (Boston, 1936), pp. 100ff.

During the late 1860s and early 1870s cattlemen not only in Texas but throughout the range country combined into close-knit associations. The local unit of the association was the round-up district, usually covering approximately 2,000 square miles. Dates were set for the spring and fall roundups, and where several brands were using the same range, owners were denied the right to gather their cattle at any other time. No general ever controlled the movements of an army more rigidly than the roundup committees controlled the movements of men and cattle during the roundup. Territorial and state associations undertook a variety of activities, including the employment of brand inspectors or detectives at the shipping centers and the maintaining of lobbies at the capitals.

In 1869 the range industry was still in the hands of the men who had pioneered it. By 1880 absentee and even alien ownership was a conspicuous feature of the cattle business. Eastern and British corporations became members of the associations by buying herds and range rights from the pioneers. In the Northwest they secured control of these organizations and used them to establish a monopoly of public grass by denying others membership in the associations. "Of course," wrote E. V. Smalley in 1885, "there is no legal power to keep out new men who may wish to bring in cattle, but such men would be boycotted by not being allowed to participate in the roundups, by having their mavericks taken as the property of the association, and by being annoyed in many ways by the cowboys of the old occupants of the Territory."[23]

Through the control of the cattlemen's associations in Wyoming, the corporations secured control of the territorial government and passed various laws strengthening their monopoly. Wherever they dominated the associations, they introduced other practices of capitalistic industrialism, including the use of

[23] *House Executive Documents*, 48th Congress, 2nd sess. 1884–1885, vol. 29, no. 267, p. 77.

labor blacklists and the employment of private gunmen.[24] At the same time they tried to increase their own prestige by advertising the fact that the stockman was "no longer a semi-savage adventurer" but a practical man of business.

That it was the "practical man of business" rather than the "semi-savage adventurer" who was chiefly responsible for the conflict between the small cattlemen and the settlers on the one hand and the cattle corporations on the other is shown by the divergent histories of the range industries in Texas and the Northwest. British and Eastern American corporations that had invested heavily in Texas sent their lawyers to represent them at the meetings of the Panhandle Stock Association, which had been organized under the leadership of Charles Goodnight in 1881. These servants of absentee capital proposed that the by-laws of the Association be amended so as to grant "extra votes on the basis of cattle owned." Although this amendment would have given him and his partner the most powerful voting strength in the Association, Goodnight, having grown up on the frontier, was too close to the pioneering tradition to consent to such palpable subordination of human need to wealth. "I knew nothing about oratory," [he told his biographer, J. Evetts Haley] "but I got up and told them plainly that such a move would defeat the purpose of the Association, which was to give the little man equal rights with the big man, and before I'd see such a rule passed, I'd disband the whole organization. But the rule did not pass."[25]

Not all the Texas organizations were as successful in preventing theft as the Panhandle Association was, but they all resisted control by absentee capital, and the Texas and Southwestern Associations, which resulted from the merger of the various smaller organizations, has until this day retained its

[24] Ibid. See also *Senate Documents*, 1885–1886, vol. 1 no. 34; and Osgood, *The Day of the Cattleman*.
[25] Haley, *Charles Goodnight*, p. 365.

democratic character. This democratic policy, together with the fact that the land and grazing acts passed by the Texas legislature were better adapted to popular needs than those passed by Congress, minimized the conflict between cattlemen and settlers in Texas.

The absence of a strong labor movement on the frontier is not to be attributed to individualism. The availability of land resulted in scarcity of labor that kept wages relatively high. The wage earner, until the invasion of the frontier by corporations, was in close contact with his employer: the relationship was personal, neighborly, and most often cordial; for where other employment was available a man would not long remain in the employ of a "boss" he did not like: he would "draw his time" and move on. The laborer had equal access to arms with his employer. Before there can be any serious oppression of labor there must be a well-ordered community where the oppressor is supported by a subservient police and judiciary. A frontier ballad tells what happened to one entrepreneur who in the absence of these sanctions attempted to introduce on the range a system of exploitation long in use by whaling captains and Eastern industrialists:

It happened in Jacksboro in the spring of seventy-three,
A man by the name of Crego came stepping up to me,
Saying, "How do you do, young fellow, and how would you
    like to go
And spend one summer pleasantly on the range of the buffalo?"

"It's me being out of employment," this to Crego I did say,
"This going out on the buffalo range depends upon the pay.
But if you will pay good wages and transportation too,
I think, sir, I will go with you to the range of the buffalo."

"Yes, I will pay good wages, give transporation too,
Provided you will go with me and stay the summer through;
But if you should grow homesick, come back to Jacksboro,
I won't pay transportation from the range of the buffalo."

It's now our outfit was complete—seven able-bodied men,
With navy six and needle gun—our troubles did begin;
Our way it was a pleasant one, the route we had to go,
Until we crossed Pease River on the range of the buffalo.

It's now we've crossed Pease River, our troubles have begun.
The first damned tail I went to rip, Christ, how I cut my thumb!
While skinning the damned old stinkers our lives wasn't a show,
For the Indians watched to pick us off while skinning the buffalo.

He fed us on such sorry chuck I wished myself most dead,
It was old jerked beef, croton coffee, and sour bread.
Pease River's as salty as hell fire, the water I could never go—
O God! I wished I had never come to the range of the buffalo.

Our meat it was buffalo hump and iron wedge bread,
And all we had to sleep on was a buffalo robe for a bed;
The fleas and gray-backs worked on us, O boys, it was not slow,
I'll tell you there's no worse hell on earth than the range of
    the buffalo.

Our hearts were cased with buffalo hocks, our souls were cased
    with steel,
And the hardships of that summer would nearly make us reel.
While skinning the damned old stinkers our lives had no show,
For the Indians waited to pick us off on the hills of Mexico.

The season being near over, old Crego he did say
The crowd had been extravagant, was in debt to him that day—
We coaxed him and we begged him and still it was no go—
We left old Crego's bones to bleach on the range of the Buffalo.

No formal organization of buffalo hunters was needed for con-
certed action in an instance like this.

That the cowboy was capable of working in harmony with
his fellows is shown not only by the highly cooperative nature of
his work, but also by a strike which occurred in the Texas Panhandle in 1883. No representative of the Knights of Labor or
other outside agitator had visited the region. Out of the casual
talk of a group that had met in a dugout came the decision to

demand an increase in pay from $30 to $50 a month. The demand was placed in writing and submitted to the managers of five large ranches. Provision was made for paying the board of any strikers without funds. While there was newspaper talk of grass-burning and fence-cutting, there was no disorder nor fear of disorder on the range; no threat of violence was implied in the "ultimatum" drawn up by the leaders of the movement. The members of the association merely bound themselves not to work for less than $50 a month and stated that "anyone violating the above obligations shall suffer the consequences." After twelve days they won their demands. According to the Bureau of Labor Statistics, 325 men were involved. Testimony from the range, however, indicates that the number participating in the strike was much smaller and that the cowboys regarded their action a good joke on the owners. Evidently they felt no deep grievances, for they made no attempt to set up a permanent bargaining agency to maintain the wage scale and regulate working conditions.[26]

When, however, progress with its attendant increase of corporate industry made it impossible for the laborer to meet his employer man to man—to secure redress of grievances by direct conference and action, labor on the frontier was no more reluctant to organize and bargain collectively than labor elsewhere.

Contrast the experiences of Herman Melville and Mark Twain. What Melville's earnings would have been if he had not deserted his whaling ship, I do not know. If he had received the average "lay" of men in the industry, and if the *Acushnet* had had average success in taking whales, his pay would have been about nineteen cents a day. Much of this would have been absorbed by debits. For example, if he had required a reefing jacket from the ship's commissary, he would have been charged $5 for

---

[26] My own researches have been supplemented by those of Professor Ruth Allen of the University of Texas and her associate, Mr. Ben Owens, who have kindly allowed me access to their files.

a garment that had cost the owners $2.50. If he had drawn $7.50 for shore leave, his debit would have been $10.00. Moreover he witnessed the flogging of men for the most trivial offenses, a form of brutality which continued even after the prohibitory statute of 1850.[27] When Samuel Clemens finished his apprenticeship, he could boast that "a pilot, in those days, was the only unfettered and entirely independent human being that lived on this earth." He was about the only person who "failed to show, in some degree, embarrassment in the presence of foreign princes."[28] And a pilot's salary was commensurate with his dignity and importance. Clemens began at $250 a month; before the river closed in 1861, this figure had been doubled.

There was no whalers' union. But the steamboat pilots on the edge of the frontier had organized what was "perhaps the compactest, completest, and strongest commercial organization ever formed among men."[29] Although the history of this organization is told in Mark Twain's *Life on the Mississippi*, and should be universally known, it has been generally ignored by writers on frontier individualism. The pilots found that wages were falling as a result of their having trained too many apprentices. They organized and agreed to control apprenticing through their association. They demanded a wage of $250 a month, and provided unemployment benefits of $25 a month for their members and a like income for widows. The organizers were promptly discharged, but the owners were eventually brought to terms, partly by the intervention of the underwriters, who noted that accidents were rare on boats piloted by union members, but common on boats not so piloted. A completely closed shop was established, and when the pilots announced that after September 1, 1961, wages would be advanced to $500 a month, the owners acquiesced, and the captains took steps toward organizing an associa-

[27] Elmo Paul Hohman, *The American Whaleman* (New York, 1928).
[28] Mark Twain, *Life on the Mississippi* (New York, n.d.), p. 119.
[29] Ibid., p. 127.

tion of their own. The Civil War and railroad competition prevented the maturing of this movement.

It is significant that the first victory which labor won in its struggle with the railroads was won in the Southwest, a region which in 1885 was close to the frontier. Jay Gould, who had crushed labor on the Erie and other systems under his control, attempted to apply the same tactics to the unionized Missouri Pacific and Texas and Pacific. In the region traversed by these roads he found public opinion strongly against him. True he was supported by the daily press, but the country weeklies, representing more accurately the attitudes of the folk, were loud and all but unanimous in the denunciation of the railroad management and in the support of the Knights of Labor. Public officials were unawed; the governors of Texas and Missouri refused to call out the militia to suppress the strike, and Gould was forced to come to terms. The next year, however, through his receiver Brown, he repudiated his agreement of 1885. He had in the meantime secured the appointment of one of his henchmen, a lawyer on his payroll named Pardee, to a federal judgeship in the district where he precipitated a strike by causing the discharge of a shop foreman for attending a meeting of the Knights of Labor. Labor union officials and strike leaders were jailed by the score. Farmers passed resolutions of sympathy and sent food to hungry strikers, but the strike was lost in spite of public sympathy. The evidence is convincing that Gould could not have crushed labor in the Southwest without the aid of the federal judiciary.[30]

Historians have generally assumed that the agrarian movement of the late nineteenth century was a result of the closing of the frontier. The assumption has a superficial plausibility inasmuch as the movement reached its political climax in 1896, after the frontier was officially closed. Yet there had always been an

[30] Here again I must acknowledge my obligation to Professor Allen and Mr. Owens.

agrarian movement on the frontier. The Granger cases reached
the Supreme Court in 1876, when free land was still available.
The frontiersman had always assumed that he could legislate for
the common good. If he at times complained about the federal
encroachment upon states' rights, it was because he distrusted
the class in charge of the government in Washington. He caused
his state legislatures to pass acts on all manner of subjects. In
Nebraska all male residents between the ages of sixteen and
twenty were subject to draft for fighting grasshoppers. The
plainsman had no fear that the state in asserting this control
over minors would encroach upon the prerogatives of parent-
hood.

The tendency toward minute regulation is manifest also in
Texas cattle legislation of 1874. E. J. Davis, reconstruction governor, seeking to bolster his crumbling regime, appealed for support on the frontier by allowing the cattlemen to write their own
legislative ticket. It should be remembered that the cattle corporations had not yet invaded the state and the industry was in the
hands of the pioneers. The act, approved by Davis's successor,
assigned a brand inspector to each western county. If an owner
drove horses or cattle out of the state without road-branding
them on "the left side of the back behind the shoulder," he could
be fined $100 for each animal so driven. Possession, without a
bill of sale, of any animal or hide bearing a brand other than that
of the possessor entailed a fine of $100 for each animal or hide.
A minor was prohibited from branding cattle except in the presence of his parent or guardian. Although a stockman might own
several brands, if in the original branding he used more than
one of them on the same animal, he could be fined $20. One who
sold hides without having them inspected could be fined $5 for
each hide sold.[31] It is true that these acts, originally passed at the
instance of the cattlemen, were found unduly complex and re-

[31] H. P. N. Gammel, *Laws of Texas*, Fourteenth Session, 8:34. (Austin,
1898).

strictive and were later in part repealed and otherwise simplified, but the demand for simplification was based on expediency
and not on any theory of individual liberty or upon any outcry
against regimentation.

These acts show that the pioneer was not averse to regulating
himself. The Texas railroad act of 1853, passed two years before
the general railroad act of England, is an example of his attempt
to regulate absentee-owned corporations. One group of provisions
looked toward the public safety, and was concerned with such
matters as grade crossings, drunkenness on the part of train
crews, and the like. Other sections compelled cooperation among
the different railroads, and others regulated rates. The second
group of provisions is especially significant in view of the popular belief that early railroad regulation attempted to enforce
competition. The Texas act required all roads to draw the cars
of all other roads, and the amendment of 1860 allowed any road
to draw its own cars over a road refusing to draw them. The power to fix rates was declared a function of the legislature, but
there was to be no change for ten years. At the end of that time
rates might be revised downward if profits exceeded twelve percent. This figure suggests that railroad attorneys might have had
a hand in the drafting of the act. Twelve percent, however, did
not seem an excessive profit to pioneers who were in need of railroad facilities and who were accustomed to pay two percent a
month and more on bank loans. Companies were required to
maintain offices on their main lines, and their books were to be
open at all times for inspection by the legislature. If a road became insolvent through the declaring of dividends, the directors
were personally liable for the debts of the company. A clause,
repealed in 1860, specified the terms upon which the state might
purchase the railroads. An amendment of 1860 attempted to pro-
hibit stock watering and other abuses of corporate finance by
declaring that every officer or director should be personally liable
for any stock illegally issued, and that no railroad company

should issue stock "except at par value and to actual subscribers who pay, or become liable to pay, the par value thereof."[32]

In this act there is nothing to suggest that the frontiersman believed with Cornelius Vanderbilt that a man should be allowed to do as he pleased with a railroad merely because he owned it.

The pioneer regulated private enterprise when he thought it expedient to regulate private enterprise. He cooperated with his fellows under the same conditions necessary at all times for voluntary cooperation; that is, (1) when he thought his interests would be furthered by cooperation, and (2) when a technique was proposed that he thought had a reasonable chance for success. "Interests" here includes not only economic advantage, but whatever gives the individual his deepest satisfactions, including the association with and approval of his fellows. An Indian attack on one family was an obvious menace to all families. The technique was equally obvious. You armed and drove the Indians away. During a grasshopper plague you called out the available manpower and fought the insects with whatever weapons were at hand; but in the meantime you agitated for a bureau of entomology. As the common menace became more complex, the technique became less obvious, and consequently cooperation became more difficult. As industry and transportation became national and destroyed the corporate life of the local community, frontier techniques of cooperation became less effective.

Early pioneer folkways suggest how people unconditioned by theoretical economics might react to an economy of abundance. There was on the frontier a scarcity of consumer's goods but an abundance of resources. Discoverers of placer deposits in the early days of Pacific mining rarely attempted to determine the extent of a deposit and claim the whole for themselves. Those who did attempt such monopoly did not succeed until statutory law had modified the folk law of the miners. Law and custom

[32] Texas railway legislation is summarized by C. S. Potts in *Railway Transportation in Texas* (Austin, 1909), University of Texas Bulletin 119.

in Texas assumed that equal opportunity was to be given to all who might wish to capture wild cattle and mustangs. The pioneer's cry from the beginning was for equality of opportunity to acquire land. The Jeffersonian ideal of equal rights for all, special privileges for none was only partially realized on the frontier; but it would have been more nearly realized if the pioneer had not been thwarted by Congress and the courts.

The pioneer believed in private property. Yet it is conceivable that he would have acquiesced in public ownership of land but for two potent reasons. Before universal male suffrage he could most easily acquire the status of citizen by becoming a freeholder. Then and later he had a well-merited distrust of Congress. He was eager to secure title to his land before it was given away. He did, however, socialize the mineral resources of Texas. In Texas, too, where several millions of acres of land yet belong to the state, pioneer cattle and sheepmen are content to occupy them by lease. Agitation for the sale of public land in Texas has come from the politicians who want to tax it, not from the people who occupy it.

If all this is true, why is the myth of frontier individualism so generally accepted? As I have implied, the myth springs in part from the social and economic predilections of historians. It springs in part also from the multiordinal nature of the word "individualism." The pioneer seems to have been less disposed than others to inquire into the private life of his associates, or to interfere in quarrels which he regarded as purely personal; he attached less importance to adventitious circumstances of birth and wealth; he was more tolerant of eccentricities of character; and he was more often called upon to exercise individual judgment and initiative. He was perhaps more self-reliant. But all this is not to say that he was individualistic in the sense that he eschewed collective action or advocated unrestricted individual opportunity to exploit the national resources or make money by other means.

Here is the typical *non sequitur*: The daughter of a frontiersman writes in her diary: "Father's saddle wore out, so he made
a new one out of cypress and rawhide." Now the ability to make
a usable saddle, however crude, is an evidence of resourcefulness.
Resourcefulness means self-reliance, which implies scorn for
collective action and exaltation of individual initiative. Or to
express the argument more succinctly: the pioneer made his own
saddle; therefore he believed in a laissez faire economy.

3. Frontier Humor: Despairing or Buoyant? (1942)

O ne of the most fashionable ideas which has emerged from the recent concern with American humor is the notion that the laughter of the frontier was born of despair. This bit of scholarly folklore seems to have originated with Albert Bigelow Paine; among its chief disseminators are Lewis Mumford and Van Wyck Brooks. Despite attacks on the theory by Bernard De Voto and Max Eastman, it still has wide currency among those who have accepted Herbert Hoover's distortion of Turner's interpretation of frontier history. From the hypothesis that the frontier is the source of the rugged individualism of Standard Oil, United States Steel, and General Motors, many contemporary interpreters of American life have concluded—not unreasonably—that it must have been a horrid place and that the

NOTE: Originally published in *Southwest Review* 27 (spring 1942): 320–334.

only laughter possible for a frontiersman must have been a grim release of frustrated hopes.

The scripture classically chosen for exegesis is a passage from Paine's *Mark Twain*:

> The frontier with its hardships and tragedies was little more than a vast primeval joke: when all frontiersmen were obliged to be laughing philosophers in order to survive the stress of its warfares.
>
> Western humor: It is a distinct product. It grew out of a distinct condition—the battle with the frontier. The fight was so desperate, to take it seriously was to surrender. Women laughed that they might not weep; men laughed when they could no longer swear. "Western humor" was the result. It is the freshest, wildest humor in the world, but there is tragedy behind it.[1]

It is not hard for a literary man to find good reasons why the pioneer ought to have despaired. Placing himself imaginatively in the frontier environment, the modern man of letters has no difficulty in conceiving what misery, what a sense of frustration, would have been his had he been engaged in a struggle against Indians and panthers and floods and grasshoppers and hail. Hence it must follow that the pioneer was miserable. Poor Daniel Boone, David Crockett, Kit Carson, Charles Goodnight, and the rest. They were vigorous men, given to vigorous and direct expression. But there were occasions when the customary channel of relief was blocked: and when they could not swear, they laughed, for not to swear or to laugh was to surrender.

When the literary man looks at the results of the frontiersmen's struggle, he feels that they had good cause for pessimism. They went West to become freeholders, to acquire rich land and the freedom and stability they associated with it. They hoped to

---

[1] Albert Bigelow Paine, *Mark Twain: A Biography* (New York and London, 1912), vol. 1, p. 454.

—and some of them did—endow their children with farms and ranches. But the ironical result is that some of the richest land on the continent is tilled—although of course not owned—by the poorest people. The resources of the continent went for the enrichment of the few. Baffling problems of agricultural production were solved only to create unmarketable surpluses. It is indeed doubtful whether the majority of the needy going West gained more than temporary alleviation of their poverty.

Aside from these *a priori* considerations, the laughter-of-despair theory of frontier humor has some support in the testimony of early travelers. Anthony Trollope, for example, found the men of the West "gloomy and silent—I might almost say sullen."[2] Sullen men, it is assumed, are not happy men, and a case for a tragic West seemed supported by contemporary evidence.

Such evidence, however, requires careful interpretation. Judge Hall, who knew the West better than Trollope, found that the frontiersman, "though taciturn in the presence of strangers, is communicative to his friends or guests, has often strong colloquial powers, with quaint, singular, figurative, and even eloquent forms of expression."[3] Why the traveler often found him sullen is suggested by Alexander Mackay, who accuses his fellow Englishmen of "demeaning themselves in their peregrination . . . with an ill-disguised air of self-importance, unpalatable to a people who have become jealous from unmerited bad treatment."[4]

The *Illinois Gazette*, in offering advice to those contemplating removal to the West, sounded a significant note of warning:

> No matter how poor he may be, or how much a stranger; if he makes no apologies, does not show a niggardly spirit by contending about trifles; and especially if he does not begin to

[2] Anthony Trollope, *North America* (Philadelphia, 1863), vol. 2, pp. 107–108.

[3] James Hall, *Legends of the West* (Cincinnati, 1832), vol. 1, p. xii.

[4] Alexander Mackay, *The Western World* (London, 1851), vol. 3, p. 322.

dole out complaints about the country and the manners of the people, and tell them of the differences and superiority of these things in the place whence he came, he will be received with blunt, unaffected hospitality. But if a man begin by affecting superior intelligence and virtue, and catechising the people for their habits of rough simplicity, he may expect to be marked, shunned, and ridiculed with some term of reproach.[5]

It may be argued also that the extravagant burlesque of the outsider's conception of the frontier—this implicit repudiation of the canons of gentility—is itself a gesture of despair. Here is a tobacco-chewing barbarian. He knows that he can never attain the drawing-room refinement of a Captain Basil Hall. In despair he assumes "in gross form the faults with which he is charged." He boasts that he does not know what a cuspidor is for. Here is a gentleman asleep under a live-oak tree with a silk hat by his side. The silk hat is a badge of refinement, a notification to the cowboy that the sleeping gentleman has attained a Culture beyond the reach of a wandering cowherd. In despair the herdsman draws his six-shooter and destroys the hat, the symbol of his inferiority. Here is Captain Marryat, a gentleman of military bearing, a writer of genteel romances, a product of a ripe European culture, in comparison with which the Kentucky of 1837 is poor indeed. In despair the young blades of Louisville stage for his benefit a mock free-for-all, thus assuming in gross form the faults with which they are charged.

No one who has the slightest acquaintance with the oral literature of the frontier will deny that the humor is often grim. Corpses are not infrequent in the comic tales and anecdotes.

A body is discovered dangling from a cottonwood tree. Pinned to the clothing is a placard: "In some respects this is a very bad man. In other respects he is a damn sight worse."

[5] Quoted by Robert Tudor Hill, *The Public Domain and Democracy*, Columbia University Studies in History, Economics, and Public Law, vol. 38 (1910), p. 93.

A minister who attaches supernatural importance to the last words of the dying is questioning a boy about the death of his mother.

"What was the matter with her?"

"We don't know. It just seems like she kinda pined away and died."

"Was she able to speak and recognize her friends at the approach of death?"

"Yes, she spoke about a half an hour before she died."

"Indeed! And what were her last words?"

"She asked for a chaw of terbacker."

In 1846, when W. H. Milburn was on his way from Washington to Chicago with his bride, the stagecoach driver, after he had crossed a bridge during a dark, stormy night, shouted "with glee,"

> "By Jove! Weren't we lucky? A half minute more and we'd all been smashed. I never was so near going over a bridge; half an inch more and we'd been over, and then salt wouldn't have saved us."
>
> To the rather timid question of my wife, as to whether there were any more bad bridges to cross before daylight, he replied, "Oh yes, several; but you mustn't be skeered; we must all die sometime you know."[6]

The casualness with which death was talked about and joked about suggests that the pioneer anticipated H. L. Mencken in the discovery that "in point of fact, death, like love, is intrinsically farcical—a solemn kicking of a brick under a plug-hat—and most other human agonies, once they transcend the physical—i.e., the unescapably real—have more of irony in them than of pathos."[7]

Anecdotes of disillusion and even defeat, it must be confessed,

[6] H. W. Milburn, *Ten Years of Preacher Life* (New York, 1859), pp. 195–196.

[7] H. L. Mencken, *Prejudices, Fifth Series* (New York, 1926), p. 136.

are numerous, particularly from the Great Plains, where the first attempt at agricultural settlement failed.

On a bright day in July, 1874, grasshoppers appeared. They covered the buildings and the shocks of grain and filled the air. They hit the roofs like hail. They lighted on trees and broke them down with their weight. At times they were four to six inches deep on the ground. They stopped trains, and section hands were called out to shovel them off. They were especially fond of onions, which they ate down into the ground, leaving only a thin shell. One man reported that as they passed his door, their breath smelled. They drowned in creeks in such numbers that the cattle would not drink until compelled by extreme thirst. Whole fields of corn were eaten in twelve hours.[8]

Baffled farmers without reserve capital left the country; on their wagons were such signs as these:

FROM SODOM WHERE IT RAINS GRASSHOPPERS
FIRE AND DESTRUCTION
GOING BACK EAST TO VISIT MY WIFE'S RELATIVES[9]

Victims of the West Texas drought of 1886 reacted similarly. Before abandoning his house in Abilene one settler nailed this sign to the door:

> One hundred miles to water
> Twenty miles to wood
> Six inches to hell
> God bless our home
> Gone to live with the wife's folks[10]

A sign on a covered wagon read:

---

[8] Everett Dick, *The Sod House Frontier* (New York, 1938), pp. 203–206.
[9] Ibid.
[10] H. Bailey Carroll, "The Texas Collection," *Southwestern Historical Quarterly* 49 (April 1946): 621.

> Last fall come from Rackin Sack
> Got sorry and now go rackin back.[11]

One of the yarns growing out of the successive grasshopper plagues concerns a farmer who left his team standing in the field while he went for a drink. The grasshoppers arrived. He rushed back to the field, but when he got there, the grasshoppers had already eaten his team and his harness and were pitching the horses' shoes to see which should have the farmer.

A pioneer ranchman who had lost all his property through drought and adverse markets was being consoled by some friends.

"Oh, don't worry about me," he said. "When I came here fifty years ago, I had sixty-five cents and the asthma. I still have the asthma."[12]

A group of men were lounging around the courthouse square of a Western town when a covered wagon drew up and stopped at the public trough. It was pulled by a one-eyed, gotch-eared, moth-eaten mule and a bony, crumple-horned Jersey cow. The tires were tied on with thongs of rawhide and from under the tattered sheet a woman and several children stuck out their heads.

A citizen accosted the driver: "Kind of queer team you got there stranger."

"Yes," replied the driver, "they ain't very well matched, are they?"

"Heading east, I guess?"

"Yes, I recken I am."

"I recken you didn't like it so well further out?"

"Well no, not exactly. You see I bought a couple of sections of land out toward the Pecos. Moved my family out there and

---

[11] W. C. Holden, *Alkali Trails* (Dallas, 1930), p. 75.
[12] Joe M. Evans, *A Corral Full of Stories* (El Paso, 1939), p. 64.

started waiting for it to rain, which it never did. Then my stock all died except this here Jersey cow and she lived on prickly pear, and I couldn't get away.

"I knew it would rain sometime and I knew when it did these youngsters of mine would go plumb crazy. My oldest boy had seen rain one time when he was little before we went out there, but it was so long ago that he had forgot all about it.

"Bout a couple of weeks ago a greenhorn feller came out looking for land to buy. He offered to trade me this mule for one of my sections of land. Well, when we went to make out the papers, I found he couldn't read, so I jest slipped the other section into the deed too, and I been driving mighty hard so as to be a long way off when he found it out."

Another man bought land on the strength of a map and the agent's glowing description of the region. He called at the district land office to find out how to reach his newly acquired property. The clerk looked up his section and gave him the necessary directions. A week or so later the man called at the land office again.

"Have you been on your land?" asked the clerk.

"No," replied the purchaser, "I can't truthfully say that I have been on it, but I have leaned up against it."

Wisecracks and tall tales about grasshoppers, drought, and land swindles and dozens of other unpleasant things undoubtedly tell of defeated purposes and blocked objectives, and they may suggest that the frontier was a vast joke—though hardly a primeval one, since most of the suffering resulted from land policies ill adapted to the region, and were therefore man-made. But they hardly prove the prevalence of despair, unless one argues that all laughter has such a basis, a view implicit in much writing about American culture. Even before Hitler, the *Christian Century* was reminding us that "the contemporary world is not always or even in the main a joking matter," that it is "a place of present tragedy and impending catastrophe."[13] Robert Lynd believes that "when we laugh we do something that puts us on a level with the animals."[14]

Most emphatic is Donald Ogden Stewart, who believes that humor "is based on a feeling of defeat and a sense of despair," that it is "simply a man's compensation to himself for the fact that life is terrible and that there is nothing he can do about it."[15]

If all laughter is the laughter of despair, then the pioneer despaired, and there is nothing more to be said. Yet other interpreters of American culture do not hesitate to speak of the "incorrigible optimism of the frontier."[16] One of the striking proofs of Mark Twain's universality is that he can furnish ammunition for both sides: his own pessimism grows out of the stress of frontier warfares; Beriah Sellers is the typical frontiersman. It might be noted in passing, however, that Twain did not revise his opinion of the human race upward after his travels in Europe and that Sellers's English cousin, Micawber, had never been on the frontier. The most significant difference between these famous incorrigible optimists is that Micawber depended mainly upon pull, upon knowing the right people, for whatever hope he had for the realization of his rather wistful schemes, whereas Sellers staked his faith upon the development of the country, the westward course of empire. His grandiose plans were hardly more fantastic that those realized by a number of enterprising and none-too-honest Americans.

There is actually more reason to speak of the optimism of the frontier than of its pessimism. Anthony Trollope was puzzled by

[13] *The Christian Century* 49 (March 1932): 308.

[14] Robert Lynd, "Objections to Laughter," *Atlantic Monthly* 145 (March 1930): 322–411.

[15] Henry Hart, ed., *The Writer in a Changing World* (New York, 1937), p. 126.

[16] Lucy L. Hazard, *The Frontier in American Literature* (New York, 1927), p. 150.

the frontiersman's reaction to defeat. In Missouri, during the
Civil War, he encountered a man "whose furniture had been sold
to pay a heavy tax raised on him specially as a secessionist," and
who "had also been refused payment of rent due by the Government, unless he would take a false oath."

> I may presume [writes Trollope] that he was ruined in his
> circumstances by the strong hand of the Northern army. But he
> seemed in nowise to be unhappy about his ruin. He spoke with
> some scorn of the martial law in Missouri, but I felt that it was
> esteemed a small matter by him that his furniture was seized
> and sold. No men love money with more eager love than these
> Western men, but they bear the loss of it as an Indian bears
> his torture at stake.[17]

If Trollope had understood frontier mentality, he would not
have been puzzled by the Missourian's attitude. For the pioneer
regarded no defeat short of death as final. As long as there was
a frontier, there was, as he thought, opportunity. When Crockett's gristmill washed away, he "went ahead" with a new venture. When his Whig politics turned his constituents against
him, he could tell Tennessee to go to hell; he would go to Texas.
When Goodnight's banking business failed at Pueblo, he came
to the Texas Panhandle to establish a ranch. One pioneer cattleman remarked that he had gone broke every year but one since
he had been in business. In 1886 he went broke twice. Men do
not shoot themselves nor long despair over defeats they regard
as temporary.

No observant traveler in the nineteenth century could fail
to note the frontiersman's enthusiasm for democracy, the most
important source of his optimism. This enthusiasm often took
the form of blatant boasting and belittling of England, and was
understandably offensive to British subjects. Alexander Mackay, however, with more insight than many of his countrymen,
has made a penetrating comment:

[17] Trollope, *North America*, vol. 2, p. 108.

The man whose attachments converge upon a particular spot on earth is miserable if removed from it, no matter how greatly his circumstances otherwise may have been improved by his removal; but give the American his institutions, and he cares little where you place him. In some parts of the Union the local feeling may be comparatively strong, such as in New England; but it is astonishing how readily even there an American makes up his mind to try his fortunes elsewhere, particularly if he contemplates removal merely to another part of the Union, no matter how remote, or different in climate and other circumstances from what he has been accustomed to, provided the flag of his country waves over it, and republican institutions accompany him in his wanderings.

Mackay goes on to say that America's pride in its institutions greatly contributes to the pride which an American takes in his country. "He is proud of it, not so much for itself as because it is the scene in which an experiment is being tried which engages the anxious attention of the world."

He feels himself to be implicated [continues Mackay] not only in the honour and independence of his country, but also in the success of democracy. He has asserted a great principle, and feels that, in attempting to prove it to be practicable, he has assumed an arduous responsibility. He feels himself, therefore, to be directly interested in the success of the political system under which he lives, and all the more so because he is conscious that in looking to its working mankind are divided into two great classes—those who are interested in its failure, and those who yearn for its success.[18]

Now the men who felt themselves implicated in the success of the democratic experiment, perhaps incorrectly though not illogically, accepted the criteria of success that European capitalism accepted—geographical expansion and a rising standard of living. And judged by these standards, America was succeeding

[18] Mackay, *The Western World*, vol. 3, pp. 326–328.

beyond her own dreams. The beginning of the nineteenth century witnessed the Louisiana Purchase; the middle of the century saw the establishment of our present continental boundaries; the end of the century saw all this virgin territory occupied and the frontier closed. This unprecedented expansion was inevitably reflected in popular psychology, and particularly the psychology of the frontiersman.

An expansive belief in Manifest Destiny was of course not peculiar to the West; it is reflected in the utterances of Eastern writers and statesmen as well. Whitman defined the spirit of These States, which for him included Canada and Cuba, as half love and half pride. Even the disillusioned Herman Melville wrote:

Escaped from the house of bondage, Israel of old did not follow after the ways of the Egyptians. To her was given an express dispensation; to her were given new things under the sun. And we Americans are the peculiar, chosen people—the Israelites of our time; we bear the ark of the liberties of the world. Seventy years ago we escaped from thrall; and, besides our first birth-right—embracing one continent of earth—God has given us, for a future inheritance, the broad domain of the political pagans, that shall yet come and lie down under the shade of our ark, without bloody hands being lifted. God has predestined, mankind expects, great things from our race; and great things we feel in our souls. The rest of the nations must soon be in our rear. We are the pioneers of the world; the advance-guard, sent on through the wilderness of untried things, to break a new path in the New World that is ours. In our youth is our strength; in our inexperience, our wisdom. At a period when other nations have but lisped, our deep voice is heard afar. Long enough have we been skeptics with regard to ourselves, and doubted whether, indeed, the Messiah had come. But he has come in *us*, if we would but give utterance to his promptings. And let us always remember that with ourselves, almost for the first time in the history of earth, national selfishness is unbounded philanthropy; for we cannot do a good to America but we give alms to the world.[19]

Earlier (in 1839) John L. O'Sullivan had declared that the mission of America was "to spread the four freedoms through the world—'freedom of conscience, freedom of person, freedom of trade and business pursuits, universality of freedom and equality.' " He later declared that we should claim Oregon "by the right of our manifest destiny to overspread and possess the whole continent which Providence has given us for the ... great experiment of liberty."[20]

In his Phi Beta Kappa address in 1824 Edward Everett spoke of the "perfectly organized system of liberty which here prevails,"[21] a statement only slightly qualified by his Fourth of July oration two years later, in which he said:

> The declaration of the independence of the United States, considered on the one hand as the consummation of a long train of measures and counsels—preparatory, even though unconsciously, of this event—and on the other hand, as the foundation of our constitutional system, deserves commemoration, as forming the era from which the establishment of government on a rightful basis will hereafter date. ... Thus [he concludes] was organized a family of states, associated in a confederate Union, which, if any thing human is entitled to that name, may be called a perfect form of government.[22]

George Bancroft also saw in the American experiment the hope of all mankind:

> The heart of Jefferson in writing the declaration, and of the

[19] Herman Melville, *White Jacket* (New York, 1850), pp. 180–181.

[20] Arthur M. Schlesinger, Jr., *The Age of Jackson* (Boston, 1946), pp. 427–428.

[21] Edward Everett, *Oration Pronounced at Cambridge before the Society of Phi Beta Kappa*, August 27, 1824 (Boston, 1824), p. 37.

[22] Edward Everett, *Orations and Speeches on Various Occasions* (Boston, 1853), vol. 1, pp. 111, 119.

congress in adopting it, beat for all humanity; the assertion of right was made for the entire world of mankind and all coming generations, without any exception whatever; for the proposition which admits of exceptions can never be self-evident. As is was put forth in the name of the ascendent people of that time, it was sure to make the circuit of the world, passing everywhere through the despotic countries of Europe; and the astonished nations as they read that all men are created equal, started out of their lethargy, like those who have been exiles from childhood, when they suddenly hear the dimly remembered accents of their mother tongue.[23]

Lincoln was convinced that if the United States perished, government of the people, by the people, for the people would perish from the earth.

Spread-eagle oratory was not, then, peculiar to the frontier, but as Robert Baird noted in 1832, the oratory of the Westerner was colored by the "elements of greatness" amid which he lived: "the lofty mountains on each side of the valley, the extensive inland seas on the north, the immense forests and prairies and mighty rivers. . . . But these external influences," Baird continues, "are impotent of themselves, except to excite the imagination and supply strong and appropriate similes, metaphors, and create language of wonder."[24]

Western statesmen could hardly outdo their Eastern colleagues in patriotic pride, but they could excel them in the use of vivid if often grotesque imagery. Hear Samuel C. Pomeroy of Kansas on the Oregon question:

The proudest bird upon the mountain is upon the American ensign, and not one feather shall fall from her plumage there. She is American in design, and an emblem of wildness and freedom. I say again, she has not perched herself upon Ameri-

[23] George Bancroft, *History of the United States* (Boston, 1861), vol. 70, pp. 472–473.

[24] Robert Baird, *View of the Valley of the Mississippi* (Philadelphia, 1832), pp. 92–93.

can standards to die there. Our great Western valleys were never scooped out for her burial place. Nor were the everlasting, untrodden mountains piled up for her monument. Niagara shall not pour her endless waters for her requiem; nor shall our ten thousand rivers weep to the ocean in eternal tears. No, sir, no. Unnumbered voices shall come up from the river, plain, and mountain, echoing the songs of our triumphant deliverance, wild light from a thousand hill-tops will betoken the rising of the sun of freedom.[25]

In 1852 the Honorable Richard Yates of Illinois spoke as follows in the House of Representatives:

Mr. Chairman, the population of the Valley of the Mississippi already constitutes more than one third of the entire population of the Union. And, sir, the time is not distant when the seat of empire, the stronghold of numerical power, will be west of the Alleghanies. The handwriting is on the wall. It is *manifest destiny*, sir. . . . Within the last five years three new States have been added to the Union, and there is territory at the head of the Missouri and the Arkansas, the Territories of Nebraska, New Mexico, Utah, and Oregon—and the vision of an ocean-bound Republic is now a reality. Sir, what a mighty theater for American enterprise! What a mighty course for a race of democratic liberty.[26]

Joseph C. Guild, who had grown up on the frontier in Tennessee, was expressing the sentiments of his generation when on the occasion of the laying of the cornerstone for a new courthouse on July 4, 1877, he declared:

From the thirteen States, occupying the Eastern shores of the Atlantic, containing a population of three millions, westward the star of empire has taken its way, and our republic is

[25] Quoted by H. L. Mencken, *The American Language*, 4th ed. (New York), p. 136.

[26] Quoted by B. A. Botkin, *A Treasury of American Folklore* (New York, 1944), pp. 283–284.

now bounded on the East by the Atlantic, on the South by the Gulf of Mexico and on the West by the golden shores of the Pacific, already numbering thirty-seven sovereign States, with a teeming population of forty millions; a republic unparalleled in the greatness of its extent, and unequalled in the wisdom, justice, and humanity of its institutions. For this great heritage we are indebted to Washington and his noble compatriots. "As an eagle stirreth up her nest, fluttereth over her young, spreadeth abroad her wings, taketh them and beareth them on her back," so Washington encouraged and led his people to victory and to glory. When did power ever lose its iron grasp, but as that grasp relaxed in death? The brow of man and lovely woman, once lifted up in sacred freedom to heaven, will never again willingly bow down in galling servitude. Let man but once taste the morsel of his birth-right, and he will purchase with his life-blood its minutest crumb. The glorious principles announced in the Declaration of Independence were borne to final triumph through scenes which should live forever in all generous hearts, and the men who supported them by their lives and fortunes, deserve to stand in the front ranks of fame's battalion, and their memory should be honored and cherished in all time to come by every devotee of liberty. Glorious era, pregnant with the destiny and liberties of man! ... Greece gave literature and Rome civilization to the world, but it was ours to give civil and religious liberty.[27]

S. S. Cox was probably parodying this address when he attributed to Guild the following effusion:

Our narrow settlements, bordering on the Atlantic, and running north to the lakes, have been in an unexampled manner extended from ocean to ocean, and State upon State has been added to the Union, with their teeming millions. "Westward the star of empire takes its way," until our eagle, grown with the dimensions of the country, rests his talons on the loftiest peaks of the Rocky Mountains, drops one pinion on the Atlantic

[27] Jo. C. Guild, *Old Times in Tennessee* (Nashville, 1878), pp. 425–426.

Ocean, bathes the other in the distant waters of the Pacific and while he is billing and cooing Cuba to come and unite her destiny with that of the United States, his tail is cooled by resting on the icebergs of the North.[28]

Spread-eagle oratory on whatever plane cannot be accounted for except as a psychological corollary of geographical expansion. Neither can the humor of the frontier. "There is," observed S. S. Cox, "a sympathy running through the American mind of such intensity and excitement in relation to our physical growth and political importance that our humor has become intensified."[29] John S. Robb had previously noted that "the nearer sundown, the more original the character and odd the expression, as if the sun, with his departing beams, had shed a new feature upon backwoods literature."[30] And Charles Wentworth Dilke had written:

> The singular wildness of Western thought, always verging on extravagance, is traceable to the width of Western land. The immensity of the continent produces a kind of intoxication; there is moral dram drinking in the contemplation of the map. No Fourth of July oration can come up to the plain facts contained in the Land Commissioner's reports. The public domain of the United States still consists of one thousand five hundred million acres; there are two hundred thousand square miles of coal lands in the country, ten times as much as in all the remaining world. In the Western territories not yet in States, there is land sufficient to bear, at the English population rate, five hundred and fifty millions of human beings.[31]

As Dilke traveled further he became even more affected by pioneer enthusiasm for vastness.

[28] S. S. Cox, *Why We Laugh* (New York, 1871), pp. 89–90.
[29] Ibid., p. 73.
[30] John S. Robb, *Streaks of Squatter Life and Far Western Scenes* (Philadelphia, 1846), p. viii.
[31] Charles Wentworth Dilke, *Greater Britain* (London, 1869), vol. 1, p. 88.

When you have once set eyes upon the never-ending sweep of the Great Plains [he exclaimed], you no longer wonder that America rejects Malthusianism. . . . Maps do not remove the impression produced by the views. The Arkansas River, which is born and dies within the limits of the plains, is two thousand miles in length, and is navigable for eight hundred miles. The Platte and Yellowstone are each of them as long. Into the plains and plateau you could put India twice. The impression is not merely one of size. There is perfect beauty, wondrous fertility in the lonely steppe; no patriotism, no love of home, can prevent the traveler wishing here to end his days.[32]

It is true that the early West produced almost no literature expressing a response to landscape. When one finds purple patches on the God-in-Nature theme in the memoirs of a frontiersman he is pretty safe in concluding that the manuscript has been tampered with. Jim Bridger wrote no pretty verses on Old Faithful; Kit Carson no sonnet on Taos Mountain; Charles Goodnight no ode to the Great Plains. W. H. Milburn in the following "splurge," which he sets down as typical of an educated Western man's " 'norating' in the social hall of a western steamboat," suggests a reason why.

Gentlemen, what is poetry, but truth exaggerated? Here it can never arrive at any perfection. What chance is there for exaggeration in the Great West, where the reality is incomprehensible? A territory as large as classic Greece annually caves into the Mississippi, and who notices it? Things, to be poetical, must be got up on a small scale. The Tiber, the Seine, the Thames, appear well in poetry, but such streams are overlooked in the West; they don't afford enough water to keep up an expansive duck-pond—would be mere drains to a squatter's preemption. I have heard frontiersmen who were poets, because their minds expanded beyond the surrounding physical grandeur. Books are not yet large enough to contain their ideas—

[32] Ibid., vol. 1, pp. 110–111.

steam not strong enough to impress them on the historic page. These men have no definite sense of limitation, know no locality—they sleep not on a couch, but upon the "government lands" —they live upon the spontaneous productions of the earth, and make a drinking cup of the mighty Mississippi. Settlements within fifty miles of them vitiate the air; life for them means spontaneity and untrammelled liberty of personal movement in space and time. Their harmony with the Nature that surrounds them annihilates the most formidable of local barriers. . . . They have an instinctive dread of crowds—with them civilization means law and calomel.[33]

Timothy Flint believed that there was "more of the material of poetry than we imagine diffused through all the classes" and that "the notion of new and more beautiful woods and streams, of a milder climate, deer, fowl, game, and all those delightful images of enjoyment, that so readily associate with the idea of the wild and boundless license of a new region" had no "inconsiderable agency in producing emigration." He was aware that "the saturnine and illiterate emigrant may not be conscious" of such motives, but neither are others always aware of "all the elements of motive that determine their actions."[34]

Flint is probably nearer the truth than Lewis Mumford, who asserts that "the Pioneer had exhausted himself in a senseless external activity which answered no inner demand except that of oblivion."[35]

As incredible as the statement will appear to the mere man of letters, I venture to assert that I have known dozens of men and women whose memories went back to the days of Indian raids, who loved the plains in spite of dust and drought and hail, the mountains in spite of wind and snow, streams in spite of floods,

[33] Milburn, *Ten Years of Preacher Life*, pp. 226–227.
[34] Timothy Flint, *Recollections of the Last Ten Years* (Boston, 1826), pp. 241–242.
[35] Lewis Mumford, *The Golden Day* (New York, 1926), p. 119.

without attempting to give their feeling verbal expression. They wrote no "Daffodils"; neither did they write a *Heart of Darkness*.

The pioneer mind was stimulated also by mechanical inventions, particularly of rapid transportation.

Captain Nicholas Roosevelt's journey from Pittsburgh, where he launched the *New Orleans* on March 17, 1811, to New Orleans, where, in spite of Indians, fire, and earthquake, he landed on January 12, is one of the marvelous sagas of American history. In their admiration for the shallow-draft river steamers, frontiersmen told how this or that pilot got lost and went up a dry stream, not knowing that he was off his course until the sun came out and dried up the dew, leaving him stranded. Dozens of explosions could not stop dangerous racing; and tales were told of cautious passengers who began by begging the captain not to race and ended by offering their cargoes of bacon and lard for fuel.

From the steamboat the frontiersman drew some of his most expressive idioms. David Crockett thus described his feelings when he discovered that his first love was engaged to marry another man:

> I saw quick enough my cake was dough, and tried to cool off as fast as possible; but I had hardly safety pipes enough, as my love was so hot as mighty nigh to burst my boilers.[36]

The observant Timothy Flint early commented upon this aspect of frontier language:

> To get ardent and zealous [he writes] is to "raise the steam." To get angry, and give vent and scope to these feelings, is "to let off steam." To encounter any disaster, or meet with a great catastrophe is to "burst the boiler." The slave cheers his oxen and horses by bidding them "go ahead." Two black women

[36] *The Autobiography of David Crockett*, with an introduction by Hamlin Garland (New York, 1923), p. 39.

were about to fight and their beaux cheered them to combat
with "Go ahead and buss a boiler."[37]

The railroads were greeted with hardly less enthusiasm than
the steamboats, but no sooner had they been built, largely with
public funds for private profit, than the frontier with good reason
turned against them. Thus while one did hear about trains that
ran so fast that when they came to a dead stop they were still
going ten miles an hour, and about the man who, just as the train
was starting, leaned out the window to kiss his wife but kissed
a cow fourteen miles from the station, most of the comic folklore
concerning railroads is derogatory to the roads. A man remarks
to a fellow passenger that he would get off and walk the rest of
the way home, but his folks wouldn't be expecting him until
train time. At a division point the new conductor threatens to
put a man off the train because he has only a half ticket. The
man's defense is that when he got on the train he was entitled to
ride on half fare. A woman passenger is seized with pains of
childbirth. The conductor reproves her for getting on the train in
"that condition." She replies that when she got on, she was not
in that condition.

The struggle with the railroads was only one aspect of the long
struggle of the frontier against special interests, a struggle that
manifested itself in a series of agrarian movements extending
from Shays's Rebellion to Bryan's free-silver campaign. These
movements, mainly political, show that the frontiersman knew
that he was being exploited and that his optimism was not "incorrigible" in the sense that it was blind and unrealistic. The in-
corrigibility, if any, consisted in his reliance upon political action, in his none too well-founded hope that lawmakers might
be induced to give him relief, and that judges might not nullify
whatever remedial laws he might induce the legislators to enact.

In spite of legal setbacks, however, the pioneer retained his

---

[37] Flint, *Recollections*, p. 78.

faith in democracy, a faith that has survived the frontier and the wars and depressions that have followed. In the period between world wars, a small minority of intellectuals, of whom Ezra Pound will serve as an example, woke up to the fact that their class and the traditions for which it stood were bankrupt. They concluded with naïve egotism that civilization was bankrupt, that the American experiment had failed, and that the laughter of the frontiersman was a confession of defeat. Defeatism has been read into American history by a defeated generation of a defeated class.

4. Gib Morgan among the Heroes (1945)

Years ago in the oil fields of West Texas I used to hear tall tales about a driller named Gib Morgan: how he built a vast hotel marvelously adapted to the southwestern climate in that every one of its hundreds of rooms had either an east or a south exposure; how he brought in a difficult well using a needle and thread for a cable and drill stem; how he had to shoot a bouncing tool dresser to keep the poor fellow from starving to death.

When I first heard these tales, I assumed that Gib Morgan was a synthetic hero of the cable-tool drillers—a creation of group imagination. But when I undertook the systematic collection of the folklore of the oil industry, I soon discovered that he was a man of flesh and blood: he had been born on a certain day and at

NOTE: Originally published in *Gib Morgan: Minstrel of the Oil Fields*, pp. 2–6. Illustrated by Betty Boatright. Publications of the Texas Folklore Society, no. 20. Austin, 1945.

a certain place; he had been a soldier and had fought in certain battles in a certain war; he had married; he had had children; he had worked in the oil fields of many states; he had retired and lived in homes for disabled veterans; he had died, leaving his tracks behind him. And before I had followed those tracks north through the Mid-Continent and Appalachian oil fields, back to his birthplace, which was also the birthplace of the oil industry, in Pennsylvania, I was convinced that I had found an American folk character of first importance.

What Paul Bunyan is to lumbering, what Pecos Bill is to the range cattle industry, what Mike Fink is to keelboating, Gib Morgan is to oil. More: he is both hero and poet, a scop who wore no man's livery, flattered no master, celebrated no deeds but his own. Both as a legendary character and as a man, he is much more vivid than these other figures, who are either outright creations of the folk mind or shadowy historical personages so surrounded by legend and so lacking in authentic documentation that their real personalities elude us. He is more like David Crockett, about whom has survived a large body of authenticated fact, another large body of popularly believed legend, and a third body of tall tales of the backwoods in which he reaches supernatural proportions.

Gib Morgan did not attain the stature of Crockett. He did not go to Congress or die in the Alamo. But he did create and disseminate an odyssey of comic folklore equal to the best in the Crockett Almanacs and superior to the best in the Paul Bunyan legend. This lore, richly imaginative and often satirical, is known in Texas, Oklahoma, Kansas, West Virginia, Pennsylvania—wherever oil is produced in the United States. It is known too, I am told, in Mexico, Venezuela, Russia, the East Indies—wherever American oil crews and technicians have gone.

Although Morgan's kinship with other American heroes of comic legend is plainly evident, he is in several respects unique.

The characteristics of the type have been ably presented by Richard Dorson, who compares the legendary Crockett with the epic heroes of antiquity.[1] The hero delights in single combat with men and beasts; he is given to boasting; he takes pride in his weapons, his horse, his dogs, his woman; he has had a remarkable birth and has exhibited precocious strength in his childhood; in the end he meets a tragic death in which he is treacherously or supernaturally slain. It might be noted too that the heroes of American comic legend are for the most part notorious wasters of natural resources.

Gib Morgan does not exhibit all of these characteristics. One striking quality of his tales is the absence of supernaturalism. He was not a giant and made no pretense to the mastery of cosmic forces. This may be the result of the limitations he placed upon his imagination in making himself the hero of his tales. He was insistent upon this point. He had associates; and oil companies, notably Standard of New Jersey and Burmah Limited, figured in his narratives. But they were scrupulously kept subordinate. They were important only as stage settings and foils, only as instrumentalities through which he did his work. And since the hero was actually present in the flesh as narrator, present with his five feet, nine and a half inches of height and his hundred fifty pounds of weight, he could not be endowed with the size and strength attributed by the comic myth makers to Paul Bunyan and David Crockett. Morgan did, however, invent a giant tool dresser twenty-eight inches between the eyes and tall enough to grease the crown pulleys at the top of an oil derrick without taking a foot from the ground. But he was careful not to let Big Toolie steal his show. He made him a sort of good natured moron and eventually killed him off. So that although Tony Beaver, lumberman's hero of West Virginia took a day out of the calendar by stopping the rotation of the earth for twenty-our

[1] "David Crockett and the Heroic Age," *Southern Journal of Folklore* 6 (June 1942): 95–102.

hours, and although Crockett, alarmed one day when the sun failed to rise, investigated and found the earth frozen on its axis, thawed it out and greased the axis with bar's grease, Morgan never went for feats belonging more properly to demigods than to oil drillers.

Morgan's trade did not call for oxen, horses, guns, and the other paraphernalia of pioneer life. But he had grown up in western Pennsylvania at a time when game was abundant and horses important. The cycle of his tales shows Gib taking a day off now and then to make use of his long-range rifle, which shot salted bullets, his twenty-four-barrel fowling piece, and swift wolf hound. He had a remarkable horse twenty-two yards long with innumerable speeds forward and reverse, which served him well both on the road and on the race track.

Another striking characteristic of Gib Morgan's tales is their concern for conservation. The folk hero of the backwoods gloried in the destruction of game. The lumberman regarded it his duty to turn the forests into wastelands in the least time possible. It is a matter of historical fact that the pioneer oil industry was as wasteful as any. Not only was the recovery of underground oil inefficient, but gas was allowed to escape into the air, oil was permitted to flow into creeks killing fish and ruining land; and it was not unusual to open a casing head and allow a gusher to spout as a spectacle to entertain the public or to induce them to invest in the oil stocks. Gib Morgan was ahead of his time. He did not boast of gushers which sprayed the moon; he boasted of those he brought in and capped without spilling a drop.

Nor do Morgan's tales glorify fighting. He was not a boasting rip-snorter, half horse half alligator, a wolf with a barbed wire tail. In the cycle of his yarns there is only one account of a physical combat. It is burlesque of a high order, the story of a fight to end all fights.

The Morgan of the tales is not a wholly consistent character. Sometimes he does not appear any too bright; sometimes he is merely the witness of a strange wonder. But most of the time the trait chiefly emphasized is ingenuity. He is confronted with a difficult technical problem. After due meditation and perhaps some trial and error, he hits upon a solution so simple that he wonders that he has not thought of it before.

Not all of Gib Morgan's tales were original. Some of them have no relation to the oil industry and were traditional in the western Pennsylvania in which he grew up. These concern chiefly hunting and fishing and planting. One, the story of the bears eating the horses, is clearly an adaptation from Munchausen. Others, like those of the bouncing tool dresser, involve common motives, although I suspect Morgan's tale antedates its analogues, for he was a driller when rubber boots made their first appearance in the oil fields. Gib Morgan did not create his tales from nothing. But when due allowance has been made for borrowing and adaptation, he remains the most fertile creator of comic folk tales known to America.

In spite of the excellence and wide distribution of his tales, Morgan, the hero of them, is hardly known except among a generation of oil workers becoming fewer each year. One reason for this fact is his chronological position. The Bunyan legend has been in the making since some of Paul's exploits got into print in a booklet printed as advertising by the Red River Lumber Company in 1914. Writers were soon on Bunyan's trail and by the middle twenties he was known all over America. Scholars soon afterwards unearthed the Crockett Almanacs published between 1830 and 1860 and brought the Crockett of comic legend to the attention of the public. Walter Blair and Franklin Meine have combed libraries for the legends of Mike Fink. Gib Morgan came between the periods most assiduously worked by the folklorists. He was already known among oil field workers as the Munchausen of the oil fields in 1880. His fame reached its height about 1909. This period has been comparatively neglected by those who have been searching for native American folk humor. De-

spite its tremendous social and economic significance, the oil
industry has not appealed to the popular imagination as lumbering, mining, pioneering and cattle raising have. Drilling an oil
well, even a gusher, has seemed less spectacular than felling a
forest, fighting a panther with a butcher knife, or turning a
stampeding herd of cattle.

As Gib Morgan's fame declined he was in many places supplanted by Paul Bunyan. Most cable-tool drillers who were ac-
tive before the First World War can tell you about Gib Morgan.
Most younger ones cannot. But they will tell you tales that Gib
Morgan told and will attribute his exploits to Paul Bunyan. This
process of substitution, in which one hero gets the edge on another and gradually displaces him, is familiar to every folklorist.
And the reasons for Bunyan's edge are fairly obvious. Lumber is
more widely distributed than oil, and therefore the lumber hero
is more widely known. In addition, Bunyan had excellent press
agents in Esther Shephard and James Stevens, and in the 1920s
young book-reading oil workers, especially college men during
summer vacation, carried his name into the oil patches in which
they worked. Paul Bunyan had not long been before the public
when journalists, feeling the need for some American super-
lative, made his name a common adjective. Thus an unusually
large electric motor is referred to as a Paul Bunyan motor and a
task requiring great strength or effort is called a Paul Bunyan
job.

Gib Morgan has not become a household word. But any cable-
tool driller who learned his trade in Pennsylvania, West Virginia or Ohio before the First World War knows that after all Paul
Bunyan is a mere lumberjack who has never been near an oil
well and who wouldn't know a Samson post from a headache
post if he had. The real hero of the oil fields is Gib Morgan.

Gib Morgan's tales, however, transcend the oil industry.
Created at a time when a resource hitherto unutilized and scarce-

ly known was being spectacularly exploited, they symbolize the whole era of expanding geographical and industrial frontiers, the era of manifest destiny and spread-eagle oratory, the era in which the folk artists, as distinguished from the literary artists, in response to a deep social urge attempted to create a literature commensurate with the events of the times.

5. The Art of Tall Lying (1949)

The tall tale has come to be accepted as one of the most characteristically American forms of folk humor. Folklorists have for a number of years been collecting the tales, anthologists have been putting them into books, and professional writers have been imitating them. Interest in the tall tale is not diminished by the fact that the conditions under which it arose are rapidly passing away. Its discovery by the public is probably a result of an unconscious search for cultural roots in the past.

The age of spread-eagle oratory, of manifest destiny, of steamboat navigation and railroad building, when the nation seemed less modest in its ambitions than the land-hungry settler who declared he would be content to acquire merely the land adjoining his own land and the land adjoining the land adjoining his own, when men who failed in business might yet hope for a new

Note: Originally published in *Southwest Review* 33 (August 1949): 357–362.

start on the frontier, when natural resources, though being wasted at a tremendous rate, yet seemed inexhaustible, when the population was expanding over a continent where everything seemed colossal—this age and this continent demanded a popular literature of heroic proportions, one which the professional men of letters could not supply.

The men who went west and fought Indians against heavy odds, who on occasion engaged panthers and grizzly bears with bowie knives, who saw forty thousand mustangs in a single drove, who estimated the herds of migrating buffalo at from three to twelve millions—these men of action would not have been greatly interested in Emerson's transcendental speculations, Whitman's glorification of the divine average, Longfellow's poetic epics, and the other effusions of the whiskered poets if they had had access to them.

It was not that the frontiersmen were universally unlettered. Many of them were emphatically not so. It was that the facts surrounding them, their own experiences, were more intense than anything they could have read.

Frontier editors were aware that there was no adequate literature of the frontier. Such outbursts as that of the *Texas Mercury* for April 22, 1854, were not uncommon.

In no country [the editor declared] are the elements of poetry found more abundant that in America. Here nature is on the grandest scale. A Niagara, with its majesty, is calculated to excite the imagination, and inspire with grandeur the conceptions of the most unimaginative mind. The majestic streams, for ever losing themselves in the bosom of the ocean; the mountains whose summits mingle with the sky; the wide-spread prairies, at the proper time carpeted in green, and suggestive of another Eden, and, at others, bleak and desolate as the sandy plains of the Sahara: all these would intimate that man should excel his predecessors in the old world as they surpass it in natural beauty.

Then there were the Indians, or the "aborigines," as the editor preferred to call them, "fading before the face of civilization as the dewdrop under the scorching rays of a vertical sun," whose history was "replete with a melancholy interest, which should strike the most careless observer." Much more in the same vein. The editor thinks that our failure to achieve a literature in keeping with these grand themes is "owing to the utilitarian tendencies of the age"— a threadbare view still maintained by numerous bookish critics. A sounder explanation is suggested by the editor's own diction.

Literary men of the frontier from Timothy Flint and James Hall to Hamlin Garland were as emphatic as the country editors in their insistence that the frontier abounded in materials suitable for great art. They further insisted that only those who knew the West at first hand should essay to use these materials, and they intimated that the literature should differ in kind as well as substance from that appropriate to the Atlantic states. Yet when they ceased to theorize and began to practice, they proved themselves hardly less slaves to the traditions of another culture than did the editor quoted above. Flint wrote in the manner of the European romanticists; there was more of Dickens than of California in the tales of Bret Harte; and Garland wrote significant fiction only when he forgot about art in the heat of social indignation.

But the westward-moving men of action, unhampered by any high-falutin theories of art, created their own literature. The pathos and tragedy of their experience they recorded in their songs; their zest for the hard life of the frontier in their prose tales. Had they lived in a prescientific age, they might have produced an *Odyssey*, or more probably a *Beowulf*. Since, however, the age of the serious folk epic had passed, and they were essentially realists, their heroic literature took a comic turn; and in keeping with nineteenth-century ideals, their comedy was the comedy of exaggeration. In the tall tale they developed one of America's few indigenous art forms.

For tall tale telling was an art. The frontiersman lied in order to satirize his betters; he lied to cure others of the swellhead; he lied in order to initiate recruits to his way of life. He lied to amuse himself and his fellows. He was an artist, and like all true artists he found his chief reward in the exercise of his art, however surcharged that art might be with social or other significance. Of Ovid Bolus, a character in Joseph G. Baldwin's *Flush Times of Alabama and Mississippi*, who used to stand at the edge of the blackjack thickets of central Texas and with his Colt's revolving rifle bring down the Comanches that Mustang Gray flushed, it was said: "Some men are liars from interest . . . ; some are liars from vanity . . . ; some are liars from a sort of necessity . . . ; some are enticed away by the allurements of pleasure, or seduced by evil example and education. Bolus was none of these: he belonged to a higher department of the fine arts, and to a class of professors of this sort of Belles Lettres." "A mixture of a lie doth ever add pleasure," said Bacon. Tom Ochiltree, Texas plainsman, said just as profoundly that he had rather lie on credit than tell the truth for cash.

If one doubts that tall lying is an art, he has but to hear the oral yarns of a gifted raconteur and then read the imitative efforts of an ungifted writer. For the benefit of such writers I set down some principles I have learned by listening to the talented frontiersmen of the Southwest.

Contrary to the conventional analysis of American humor, the folk liar does not depend upon mere exaggeration. Exaggeration, he knows, is in itself neither folkish nor funny. No old-time cowboy would expect to amuse you by saying that the outfit for which worked owned a billion acres of land, as gross an overstatement as that would be. He would say that they used the state of Arizona for a calf pasture; that it took three days to ride from the yard gate to the front gallery; that the range reached so far that the sun set between headquarters and the west line camp. The folk humorist did not say of a hero that he had the strength of ten either because of his pure heart or because of his impure whiskey. He detailed concretely what the hero would do: he would fight a rattlesnake with his bare hands and give the snake three bites to start with. The roughneck of the oil fields did not say that Gib Morgan built a derrick five hundred miles high. He said that the derrick was so high it took a man fourteen days to climb to the top of it. A crew of thirty men was required in order to have a man on duty at all times. There were at any given time fourteen men going up, fourteen men coming down, a man at the top, and a man off tower (i.e., off shift). There were dog houses built a day's climb apart for the men to sleep in on their way up and down. The folk liar had no metaphysic of humor, but he knew that he need not expect much response from his hearers if he merely said that his hero was forty feet tall. He knew that he must provide ludicrous imagery, an ingenious piling up of epithets, a sudden transition, a *non sequitur*—something besides mere exaggeration if his audience was to respond to his tales.

Again, contrary to most academic analyses, the folk artist knew the value of understatement and used it skilfully in his boasts and in his narratives of fact and fiction. When he found himself surrounded by Indians, he was not scared: he just didn't know where to get. W. S. James thus speaks of the decline of cattle rustling in the 1890s:

> It is now getting to a point, has been for several years, that jurists and judges are getting so incredulous that the boys [who steal cattle] have been having considerable trouble to explain their mistakes, and the consequence is that many of them have been sent east to work under the supervision of the State; this is invariably done under protest, and nearly every one who

takes a state contract is innocent; and if you don't believe it, you may be convinced by going to Rusk, Texas [where the penitentiary was located] and asking them, or to the court records, and almost without exception you find a plea of "not guilty."

Some thirty years later Charley Russell in *Good Medicine* told about how Charley Cugar "quit punchin' cattle and went into business for himself. His start was a couple of cows and a work bull. Each cow had six or eight calves a year. People didn't say much till the bull got to havin' calves, and then they made it so disagreeable that Charley quit the business and is now making hair bridles. They say he hasn't changed much, but he wears his hair very short and dresses awfully loud."

"The authentic liar," says J. Frank Dobie, "knows what he is lying about." However much he may stretch the blanket he is not at liberty to lie in any way he may please. For his art is essentially realistic. His burlesque, like all good burlesque, rests on a solid foundation of truth. O. Henry declared that he might have a man stabbed with a lariat and chased by a pair of chaperros and it wouldn't be noticed until some error sharp from Mc-Adams Junction isolated the erratum and wrote to the papers about it. For the benefit of a tenderfoot an authentic liar might describe such a stabbing and such a pursuit as O. Henry mentions, but he would know what a lariat is for and what a cowboy does with a pair of chaperros. A fire-pan hunter reports that he is not having much luck with coons lately. They are getting too educated for him. When they see a light in the woods, they cover their eyes with their paws. The story would be pointless if the animal were a rabbit, say, or a deer. The teller of tall tales about the weather had better know his weather. J. Frank Dobie ridicules a writer who reported that "no old Texan would trust himself on the prairies in July or August with the thermometer at ninety-six degrees, without two blankets strapped to the saddle-bow to keep him from freezing to death should a norther blow up." As Dobie observes, "no man on the range carries his

blankets on the horn of a saddle and no Texan ever experiences a
genuine norther in July or August. The description is utterly
false, utterly lacking in authenticity."

The folk artist knows the value of circumstantial detail: perhaps just a little prefatory rambling to fix the date—yes, it was
'87, the year Roaring Springs went dry; short notes on characters—this was the same Bill Weber who took a fancy to a fine
new saddle in Peter Cowan's shop and bought it, although he had
a pretty good elum-fork, and had to sell his only horse to pay for
it; definite references to place—it was over on Brushy Creek
where Bob Ware was killed by the Comanches. There would be
enough detail of this sort to establish poetic faith, but not
enough to clog the action: the main point was never lost sight of.

For the tallest of tall tales, as distinguished from mere tall
talk, had a logic and a structure. The tall tale is logical in all
points but one. It begins plausibly and builds carefully up to a
climax, and the narrative must not topple until the climax is
reached. At the point of highest suspense there is a pause. Here
the listener is sometimes induced to ask a question. The answer
may be a sell, a notification that the hearer has been taken in,
not necessarily in the sense that he believed what has gone before, but in the sense that he has not yet discovered the catch.

One of the oldest of this type is the that's-your-lookout ending.

A man describes a dense forest. The trees were so thick that he
could hardly make his way on foot, much less on horseback.
Other details follow. Animal life abounds. It is a hunter's para-
dise. There are bears and deer, but elk are especially numerous.
Why, he'd seen hundreds with an antler-spread of fifteen feet.

"But," asks the listener, "if the timber is as thick as you say,
how did the elk get through the forest?"

"That's your lookout."

Similar is the they-got-me formula.

A man is hunting in the mountains. He sights a bighorn

sheep and follows it around a ledge. The ledge narrows until it is not more than a foot wide. He looks down and sees a bluff five hundred feet to the bottom of a stream, and he looks up and sees a bluff five hundred feet to the top of a mountain. At a diffcult place he stumbles and drops his rifle, and being without arms, he starts back to camp. He rounds a bend and finds a mountain lion creeping toward him. He turns around and finds his path blocked by a grizzly bear. How did he get off? He didn't get off. They got him, but whether it was the bear or the cougar, he never did find out.

Another tale of this type represents the narrator as being chased by a bear into a cave occupied by a panther, another as fleeing up a canyon to escape a band of yelling Comanches and meeting a war party of Apaches. Any devil and deep blue sea will do.

The less-than-to-be-expected ending is exemplified by a tale told by a man who, according to his own testimony, had during the late unpleasantness served the Confederacy in many capacities, among them waggoner. Once, he said, he received at the railhead a consignment of powder to be transported to the front. By that time the services of supply had been rather thoroughly disorganized, so that there were no kegs or other containers at the powder mill. The powder had been shipped loose in a box car, and was shoveled into the wagon as so much sand might have been.

He received his load and started for the front where the powder was grievously needed for Lee's artillery. He had driven about two hours when he had a desire to smoke. He lit his pipe, and forgetting what sort of load he carried, he threw the still burning sulphur match down in the wagon.

Here came the pause. One listener expected to hear that the match went out, another that the speaker was blown to the moon. But the narrator was too much of an artist to say either of these things. What he said was—

"And you can hang me for a horsethief if I didn't burn up two and a half bushels of powder before I could put the fire out."

Another type of story solves an impossibility by introducing a new and grosser impossibility.

One of the old JA hands went to Arizona and acquired a small ranch on the rim of the Grand Canyon. One day, he said, he was riding along the rimrock looking for steers. The fool bronc he was riding, just out of pure orneriness he reckoned, bogged his head and began pitching. The next thing he knew they had gone off the precipice. Well, when that horse hit the bottom, he just naturally spattered all over the scenery.

What happened to the rider?

Well, when they went off that rimrock together he knew that that saddle he had been trying so hard to stay in was no place for him; so he got off, and he had to be damn quick about it, for he wasn't more than off the brute till he hit the bottom.

Another pattern involves the confirmation of the lie by a second speaker, who may either rationalize the tale or cap it.

One such yarn is reported by J. Mason Brewer in his *Juneteenth*. Jim Flant was a noted blanket stretcher who always called on his slave Abraham to verify his yarns. Flant told about a hunt he had taken Abraham on. They hunted all day without seeing any game, but as they were about to go home a big buck came out of a thicket and rushed toward them. Flant fired and the deer fell dead. Upon examination, they found that the bullet had first gone through his ear, then through his hind foot, then through his head. When this statement was doubted, Flant called on Abraham to tell how it was done. He thought a moment and then said, "Well, you see it was like this. When Massa shot him he was scratching his ear with his hind foot."

Capping a tale not infrequently takes the form of telling a bigger lie on the same theme.

A man camping out wakes during the night to find something cold and heavy on his chest. As he stirs he hears the whir of a rattlesnake, and in the dim moonlight he sees a blunt head with fangs spread ready to strike. He knows that any sudden movement would be fatal. Very quietly he moves his hand toward his six-shooter, always placed within convenient reach. The snake is drawn into an S, head erect. The man's hand closes on the butt of the six-shooter. He draws and fires just as the head is darting toward his face.

That reminds a hearer of an experience he had out on the Pecos in '83. He woke up in exactly the same fix, except, fool-like, he had forgot to put his gun where it would be handy.

What did he do?

Well, seeing there wasn't anything he could do, he just shut his eyes and went back to sleep.

Folk tales tend to cluster around certain heroes. Thus Peter Cartwright in his *Autobiography* complains that "almost all those various incidents that had gained currency throughout the country, concerning Methodist preachers, had been located on me, and . . . when the congregation came to hear me [in Boston], they expected little else than a bundle of eccentricities and singularities; and when they did not realize according to their anticipations, they were disappointed." Cartwright filled his next sermon with western anecdotes and the Bostonians were pleased. In other words, he assumed the role that folklore demanded of him and thus accelerated the process of unification.

But the accretion of folk tales around a few names is mainly the work of writers, not the folk. Crockett becomes famous as a hunter and backwoods politician, and this makes him a suitable peg upon which to hang a host of anecdotes originally attributed to others. Mike Fink attains notoriety as a fighting keelboatman. Humorists supplying copy for newspapers, almanacs, and thrillers assign to him any traditional adventure they consider to be in character. Blair and Meine in their book on Fink carry the process farther. Pecos Bill, put in print by Edward O'Reilly in

1923, though not generally accepted by actual cowboys, has become to outsiders the hero of the cattle country. John Henry was mainly a creation of Roark Bradford.

The process may be illustrated by a series of tales about a Texas ranch cook. Until recently the fame of Jim Baker, better known as Pie-Biter, depended upon a single incident. He was inordinately fond of pie and would eat several pies at one meal. Soon he began stacking one pie upon another and eating them simultaneously—first two, then three, and then four. Finally he declared that he could bite through five pies at once. He was challenged, bets were placed, and a day was set for the demonstration. Ranch hands gathered from miles around to see him make the attempt. With much effort he stretched his mouth to encompass the five pies; but he lost his bet, because he had forgotten to remove the tin plate from under one of the pies.

To this folk anecdote writers have added other folk anecdotes. Since Pie-Biter was a camp cook he becomes by substitution the hero of the following yarn earlier associated with a Texas Ranger named Deane.

It is time to prepare supper but there is no fuel: no wood, no buffalo chips, no cow chips available. The Ranger has been separated from his company and has shot a buffalo; the camp cook is with his chuck wagon. It is fall and the prairie grass is tall and dry. The grass is fired. As the fire advances, the Ranger follows with his buffalo steak on his ramrod; the ranch cook with his pots and pans. When supper is ready Pie-Biter finds no one there to eat it. He had run with the fire and by the time the meal is cooked, he is eight miles from camp. The Ranger has a day's walk getting back to his saddle animal and pack horse.

What would have happened if the heroic age in America had lasted another century, I shall not undertake to say. It may be noted, however, that since the pioneer, instead of writing books, told his tales orally as occasion arose, he did not feel a need for unification around a single character. When he told his narratives of ingenious escapes and hair-raising adventure, he might invent the name of the hero on the spot; he might ascribe the feats of daring to some local character; but he was more likely to appropriate the honors himself. The best yarns are in the first person.

6. The American Myth Rides the Range: Owen Wister's Man on Horseback (1951)

If, while you were in your neighborhood grocery this morning, or any morning this year, you went to the rack and picked up at random a two-bit novel, the chances are one in five that the novel was a western. If you read the comic strips in your daily paper, in at least one and possibly four you followed the adventures of a man on horseback. If you looked over the offering on your magazine stand, you probably saw no fewer than twenty-five of the fifty or more pulpwood magazines and a dozen of the twenty or more comic books devoted exclusively to westerns. If you read all of any issue of the *Saturday Evening Post*, the chances are six out of ten that you read either a western short story or an instalment of a western serial. If you listened to your radio all day, you heard at least one western drama, and if you sat by your

NOTE: Originally published in *Southwest Review* 36 (summer 1951) 157–162.

television set, you saw one. If you dropped into a movie house at random, the chances are one in four that you saw a horse opera.

One reason why the cowboy is a popular hero is that historically he possesses the qualities of which folk heroes are made. These qualities are two: prowess and cleverness. It is not necessary that both inhere in the same individual, but I know of no hero in any culture who has not exhibited at least one of them. Prowess, when accompanied by the virtues of bravery, skill, and loyalty, is a romantic ideal, aristocratic in its indifference to material gain, and, incidentally, accessible only to those who have economic security or are indifferent to it. An admiration for prowess thus qualified is an evidence of idealism. Cleverness is the defense of the weak against the strong, the practical against the ideal. It is the middle class's weapon against the aristocracy, the slave's weapon against his master. It is realistic and often cynical. In the folklore of the United States prowess is associated with the South, cleverness with the North.

The cowboy in the time of the open range and the overland drive exhibited both these traits. One of the few safe generalizations that can be made about cowboys is that they had the stamina and the skills necessary to the practice of their trade. They were not afraid of horses and cattle; they were willing to risk their lives in controlling stampedes and in fording rivers, and in protecting their bosses' herds against Indian raiders, Mexican bandits, and Anglo-American rustlers. In these things cleverness was as important as strength: often the best strategy was not to fight your enemy but to outwit him.

But it was not until the heroic age of the cattle industry had closed that the cowboy emerged as a national folk hero. For qualities alone do not create folk heroes. Essential also is a troubadour, or perhaps a number of troubadours. Their function is not merely to publicize the hero. More importantly it is to develop myths about him and to assimilate these myths to the archetypical myths of the culture. A myth cannot flourish without a congenial climate of opinion. In contemporary civilization the troubadours are historians, biographers, journalists, novelists, script writers. Their media are the written and spoken word, sound effects, the visual image. Their instruments are books, magazines, movies, radio, television.

Owen Wister was not the first troubadour of the cowboy, but he was the first to get a national hearing and to make his heroes acceptable to gentility. When Wister's first western story appeared in 1891, Charlie Siringo's realistic biography was being ignored in literary circles. Several dime novelists had discovered the cowboy, but had referred him to a waning mythology. To some, because he was far away from the corrupting influences of civilization and close to nature, he was innocent and good. To some, he was the contemporary knight-errant, wandering through the cattle kingdom righting wrongs with no thought of material reward. Others believed that men removed from the refinements of urban life and the restraints of home life and religion necessarily degenerated. To them the cowboy was essentially a barbarian whose only recreations were physical violence and drunkenness.

Wister attempted a synthesis of all these concepts, throwing the chief emphasis upon chivalry. His cowboys are neither Arcadian innocents nor drunken rowdies. They are natural gentlemen. Looking on the scene of the Medicine Bow saloon, he is moved to write:

> Saving Trampas, there was scarce a face among them that had not in it something very likable. Here were lusty horsemen ridden from the heat of the sun, and the wet of the storm, to divert themselves awhile. Youth untamed sat here for an idle moment, spending easily its hard-earned wages. City saloons rose into my vision, and I instantly preferred this Rocky Mountain place. More of death it undoubtedly saw, but less of vice, than did its New York equivalents. And death is a thing much cleaner than vice. Moreover, it was by no means vice that was written upon

these wild and manly faces. Even where baseness was visible, baseness was not uppermost. Daring, laughter, endurance— these were what I saw upon the countenances of the cow-boys. And this very first day of my knowledge of them marks a date with me. For something about them, and the idea of them, smote my American heart, and I have never forgotten it, nor ever shall, as long as I live. In their flesh our natural passions ran tumultuous; but often in their spirit sat hidden a true no- bility, and often beneath its unexpected shining their figures took on heroic stature.

Even the weak-minded and weak-willed Shorty is not without a touch of nobility: he loves horses. Aside from Trampas, the only Wisterian cowboy without some such touch is Hank in "Hank's Woman." "The creature we call a *gentleman*," Wister observes, "lies deep in the hearts of thousands that are born without the chance to master the outward graces of the type."

But the outward graces are important, and before Wister's cowboys can enter genteel society, they must acquire them. Even the Virginian must undergo a course in self-improvement—by reading Shakespeare and other literary classics—before he is a fit husband for Mollie Wood. And having observed the clothing of Judge Henry's eastern guests, he reaches Bennington properly attired.

The creature that we call a gentleman is above all chivalrous, and in Wister's cowboys is the chivalry of the aristocratic South modified by the West. Good women are not to be mentioned in levity. Public opinion supports the Virginian when he demands that Trampas rise up on his hind legs and admit that he has lied about Mollie Wood. A gentleman does not boast of his exploits with women not so good. The Virginian's relations with the wid- ow of medicine Bow are to be inferred from circumstantial evi- dence, not from anything he has said.

But more than gallantry, Wister emphasized the code of hon- or. After Trampas had threatened to kill the Virginian if he did not leave town by sundown, the mayor offered to put Trampas in the calaboose until the Virginian married and left town, and Lin McLean and Honey Wiggin, feeling that the code might be suspended in view of the extraordinary circumstances, offered to "take this thing off your hands." But of course it could not be. "It had come to that point where there was no way out, save the ancient, eternal way between man and man. It is only the great mediocrity that goes to law in these personal matters."

In spite of a good number of shootings, stabbings, and lynchings, physical violence is not abundant in Wister's works. His cowboys triumph by cleverness more often than by force. The Virginian outwits Trampas at every turn until the final challenge to death. In a typical Wister short story, Scipio LeMoyne recovers the payroll by giving the robber misleading directions concerning a short route to the village. His cowboys are also tricksters for fun. The Virginian got the drummer's bed by pretending that he had fits, and he got rid of the Reverend Mac-Bride by keeping him up all night on the pretense that he was about to be converted to the preacher's religion.

In Wister's cowboys, then, we have both prowess and cleverness. But more important, the Virginian exemplifies the American version of the myth of the faithful apprentice, the Horatio Alger story. Poor and obscurely born, he goes into the world— the West—to seek his fortune. He wanders from Texas to Montana and eventually settles down as a cowhand on the Sunk Creek Ranch in Wyoming. He serves his employer faithfully, never hesitating to risk life or limb, never complaining about injustices done him, but determined to make his master see his worth. He makes his own decisions and accepts the consequences of them. When duty demands, he can hang his own friend. There is no boss's daughter to reward him with; but Mollie Wood had all the qualifications except the fortune, and that is taken care of by a partnership in the firm, which under his management prospers when other ranches are going broke. But just in case drought or snows or adverse markets or cow thieves, or any act of God or man, should interfere with the profits of the ranch, a deposit of coal is found on the Virginian's land. This assures his ability to support Mollie in the style to which she would have been accustomed if the mills hadn't failed.

But Wister went much farther in making the cowboy a suitable hero for an industrial society.

Before Wister entered Harvard, the Great American Dream, the dream of a nation without great extremes of wealth and poverty, a nation in which all men might enjoy a comfortable living, had been shattered by sectionalism, civil war, and the rise of a socially irresponsible plutocracy. In the light of plain fact, the myths that had sustained unregulated business enterprise melted away. Carnegie's attempt to revive in modified form the religious sanction of stewardship was not conspicuously successful, even among his fellow millionaires. And classical economic theory, which made this the best of all possible worlds because it was a self-regulating world, in which, barring human interference, private selfishness would produce public good, was put to a severe strain. It was difficult for the farmers and laborers to understand that their impoverishment was for the greater glory of the nation.

Clearly, a new mythology was needed. It came as soon as the leaders of American opinion had time to turn from war to peace. Its chief prophet was Herbert Spencer, who, even before the publication of *The Origin of Species*, made a travesty of Darwin's biology by applying it to society and arriving at the conclusion that the rich deserved to be rich and the poor deserved to be poor. "The poverty of the incapable [he wrote], the distresses that come upon the imprudent, the starvation of the idle, and those shouldering asides of the weak by the strong, which leave many in 'shallows and miseries,' are the decrees of a large, far-seeing benevolence."

William Graham Sumner, Spencer's leading American disciple in the field of social theory, insisted that "poverty belongs to the struggle for existence" into which we are all born, and cannot be alleviated by social action. "Let every man be sober, industrious, prudent, and wise, and bring up his children to be so likewise, and poverty will be abolished in a few generations." It is not clear how the general diffusion of these qualities would lessen the intensity of the economic struggle or reduce the number of casualties, for Sumner could not conceive of a time when the contestants would be equal. "Let it be understood [he said] that we cannot go outside this alternative: liberty, inequality, survival of the fittest; not—liberty, equality, survival of the unfittest. The former carries society forward and favors all its best members; the latter carries society downward and favors all its worst members."

Theodore Roosevelt applied the theory of evolution to history in his *The Winning of the West*; Wister exemplified it in his western fiction. Indeed, a weighty element in his admiration for the culture of the cattle country was his belief that it permitted the law of natural selection to operate freely. The Virginian's comment on Shorty, who did not survive, is pertinent.

> Now back East you can be middling and get along. But if you go to try a thing on in this Western country, you've got to do it *well*. You've got to deal cyards *well*; you've got to steal *well*; and if you claim to be quick with your gun, you must be quick, for you're a public temptation, and some man will not resist trying to prove he is the quicker. You must break all the Commandments *well* in this Western country, and Shorty should have stayed in Brooklyn.

And in a passage that Spencer or Sumner might have written, Wister declares:

> All America is divided into two classes,—the quality and the equality. The latter will always recognize the former when mis-

taken for it. Both will be with us until our women bear nothing but kings.

It was through the Declaration of Independence that we Americans acknowledged the *eternal inequality* of man. For by it we abolished a cut-and-dried aristocracy. We had seen little men artificially held up in high places, and great men artificially held down in low places, and our own justice-loving hearts abhorred this violence to human nature. Therefore, we decreed that every man would henceforth have equal liberty to find his own level. By this very decree we acknowledged and gave freedom to true aristocracy, saying, "Let the best man win, whoever he is." Let the best man win! That is America's word. That is true democracy. And true democracy and true aristocracy are one and the same thing. If anybody cannot see this, so much the worse for his eyesight.

In Wister's fiction the best man wins, but in fairness to him it should be said victory is not the only evidence of the winner's superiority: it is manifest also in his physical appearance, his bearing and manner, and in his native intelligence.

The businessmen who welcomed the new theory as a weapon against social legislation felt under no compulsion of consistency to refuse the bounty of a friendly government; and Wister apparently saw nothing wrong in the cattlemen's free use of the public domain, nor in the Virginian's homesteading known mineral land.

Wister shared the contempt for the masses inherent in the doctrine of social Darwinism. This contempt is implicit in the passage about the Declaration of Independence and in story after story. In "Specimen Jones," for example, Adams has drawn a six-shooter and is making a young tenderfoot dance. "The fickle audience was with him, of course, for the moment, since he was the upper dog and it was a good show; but one in that room was distinctly against him." This one, Specimen Jones, befriends the youth and turns the crowd against Adams. Wister's exaltation of the hero at the expense of the other characters often interferes with the plausibility of his narrative. To cite one example, only the most naïve reader could believe that young Drake in "The Jimmyjohn Boss" actually intimidated the revolting cowhands and brought them to taw. This emphasis on leadership issues from something deeper than literary convention. In actual life, Wister's pathetic search for a leader brought him to the conclusion that Theodore Roosevelt was "the greatest benefactor we people have known since Lincoln."

Wister subscribed wholeheartedly to the myth of Anglo-Saxon racial superiority, which, like laissez-faire economics, had found a new sanction in the theory of social evolution. White Americans had always proclaimed the racial inferiority of Indians and Negroes and, after the frontiers met, of Mexicans. Now the doctrine was extended to all races, vaguely confused with nationalities and other cultural groups; and it was boldly proclaimed by Josiah Strong, among others, that the Anglo-Saxon race, because of its innate superiority as manifest in its genius for politics and its moral purity, was destined, under God, to rule the world. Wister approved Jim Crow legislation, and in *Lady Baltimore* attempted to establish the inferiority of the Negro on the basis of physical anthropology. Contemplating three skulls, one of a Caucasian, one of a Negro, and one of an ape, Augustus exclaims, "Why, in every respect that the African departed from the Caucasian, he departed in the direction of the ape! Here was zoölogy mutely but eloquently telling us why there had blossomed no Confucius, no Moses, no Napoleon, upon that black stem; why no Iliad, no Parthenon, no Sistine Madonna, had ever risen from that tropic mud."

Wister's admiration for Moses did not extend to contemporary Jews. His anti-Semitism is obvious in his treatment of the Jew drummers in *The Virginian* and of the Jewish student in

Philosophy Four. And in comparing Justices Holmes and Brandeis, he wrote:

> I doubt if any gulf exists more impassable than the one which divides the fundamental processes of a Holmes from those of a Brandeis:—"East is East and West is West, and never the twain shall meet." Holmes descends from the English Common Law, evolved by generations of people who have built themselves the greatest nation in a thousand years; Brandeis, from a noble and ancient race which has . . . failed in all centuries to make a stable nation of itself. *Liberty defined and assured by Law* is a principle as alien to the psychology of that race as it is native with Holmes and his ancestors.

There were Negro cowboys and Mexican cowboys, but they were few in the mountain states; and the appeal this region had for Wister was due in no small measure to the relative absence of foreigners, other than Britishers, there. In an article in *Harper's* for September, 1895, he wrote:

> Directly the English nobleman smelt Texas, the slumbering untamed Saxon awoke in him, and mindful of the tournament, mindful of the hunting-field, galloped howling after wild cattle, a born horseman, a perfect athlete, and spite of the peerage and gules and argent, fundamentally kin with the drifting vagabonds who swore and galloped by his side. The man's outcome typifies the way of the race from the beginning. Hundreds like him have gone to Australia, Canada, India, and have done likewise, and in our own continent you may see the thing plainer than anywhere else. No rood of modern ground is more debased and mongrel with its hordes of incroaching alien vermin, that turn our cities to Babels and our citizenship to a hybrid farce, who degrade our commonwealth from a nation into something half pawn-shop, half broker's office. But to survive in the clean cattle country requires spirit of adventure, courage, and self-sufficiency; you will not find many Poles or

Huns or Russian Jews in that district; it stands as yet untainted
by the benevolence of Baron Hirsch. . . . The Frenchman to-day
is seen at his best inside a house; he can paint and he can play
comedy, but he seldom climbs a new mountain. The Italian has
forgotten Columbus, and sells fruit. Among the Spaniards and
the Portuguese no Cortez or Magellan is found to-day. Except
in Prussia, the Teuton is too often a tame, slippered animal,
with his pedantic mind swaddled in a dressing-gown. But the
Anglo-Saxon is still forever homesick for out-of-doors.

Wister admits that "the Mexican was the original cowboy,"
but says that "the American improved upon him." "Soon he had
taken what was good from this small, deceitful alien, including
his name, *Vaquero* . . . translated into Cowboy."

Wister makes no direct mention of Frederick Jackson Turner.
He may have been familiar with the famous essay of 1893 in
which that historian, neglecting the presence of families and
larger social units on the frontier and minimizing the mutual
help which had made settlement possible, declared that the
frontier "promoted a democracy strong in selfishness and individualism," and "produced an antipathy to control," and in
so declaring, added, unwittingly, I think, a historical sanction to
the dialectic of American business. Spokesmen for business enterprise, accepting the Turner thesis that the frontier had been
the most important determinant in American history, and that
the frontier was opposed to social control, came to see in the
cowboy, the last of the frontier types, a symbol of the American
way. Horace Lorimer, who took over the editorship of the *Saturday Evening Post* in 1898 and frankly made it the voice of
American business, assembled a stable of western writers, including Owen Wister, and through them kept before his readers
the cowboy as a symbol of the rugged individualism that had
made America great. Henceforth the exploits of the cowboy
would recreate the tired businessman and at the same time
strengthen him in his steadfastness.

Wister made his first trip to Wyoming in the summer of 1885, when the cattle business on the crest of a boom that broke the following winter. By the time Wister got around to writing his first western story six years later, the West he had first known was gone. He never pretended that his stories described the West of the time of their writing: he always maintained that his fiction was historical. While he was writing it, he was sorely beset by three principal fears: the fear of monopoly, the fear of labor unions, and the fear of immigration. Monopolies and unions interfered with the free operation of the law of survival, and immigration threatened the Anglo-Saxon race.

> Three dangers [he wrote in *The Seven Ages of Washington* (1907)] to-day threaten the United States, any one of which could be fatal: unscrupulous Capital, destroying man's liberty to compete; unscrupulous Labor, destroying man's liberty to work; and undesirable Immigration, in which four years of naturalization are not going to counteract four hundred years of heredity. Unless the people check all of these, American liberty will become extinct.

But he had no program for checking them. Socialism, Populism, Free Silver, even the democratic liberalism of Woodrow Wilson, he hated. His social thinking was purely negative, and in his bafflement he turned to the golden age of the cattle West, an age he more created than perceived. It was not a perfect age, he admitted, but it was an uncomplicated one in which relationships were from man to man, and one in which the social myths of America might conceivably work.

There must be popular amusement—release from the tensions of modern life—and the cowboy is a hero with many faces, most of them innocent. But it is not altogether reassuring that in a time of greater complexity and greater insecurity than Wister lived to see, the cowboy with his six-shooter, his simple ethics, and his facility for direct action is our leading folk hero.

7. Aunt Cordie's Ax and Other Motifs in Oil (1953)

In all the oil regions of the United States there circulate certain archetypical stories which are told as truth and often printed in good faith, but which in many instances prove to have little or no basis in fact. Such stories are not without interest in themselves; and if they are folklore (as I believe they are) a study of their content and distribution should throw some light upon the development of folklore in a literate and increasingly industrial society. Pending a more thorough study, which must await further collecting, this paper is offered as a preliminary report on some of these tales. In it I shall deal with only three typical and widely distributed motifs.

One of these is the story of the new ax. It is meant to be comic, the humor depending upon the discrepancy between the wants and the means of the formerly poor but now rich landowner. I first heard the story in the McClesky version from Ranger, Texas.

NOTE: Originally published in *Folk Travelers*, pp. 75–85. Publications of the Texas Folklore Society, no. 25 (Dallas: SMU Press, 1953).

In 1917 Uncle John and Aunt Cordie McClesky, as their neighbors called them, were living on a farm a mile south of Ranger. They had an unpretentious but substantial farm house with a garden and orchard, for, like most of their neighbors, they produced much of their food at home. For cash income John McClesky grew cotton and peanuts, and worked as a bricklayer on the rare occasions when there were any brick to be laid in the little village. He was not used to handling large sums of money, but his condition was hardly one of poverty. The owner of property valued at some $20,000, he ranked among the more prosperous farmers of his community.

It was upon his farm that the Ranger discovery well came in on October 22, 1917, with a flush production which gave him an income of about $250 a day. Some weeks after his good fortune he built a cottage in Ranger, where the McClesky Hotel, representing the first sizable investment of his oil money, was under construction.

It was at this time that a newspaper woman from Fort Worth called upon Mrs. McClesky for an interview. The reporter quoted her as saying that when the well came in, her husband asked what he might buy for her. Mrs. McClesky replied, "Well, the blade of the old ax has a nick in it and I would like to have a new one to chop kindling with."[1]

I have heard this story in several variants (in one the handle of the ax is so old and rough that it leaves splinters in her hands) from at least a dozen informants who believe it to be true. I accepted it as truth myself until a few years ago when on the trail of Gib Morgan I found the same story in Pennsylvania. I have since heard it from Desdemona, where a farmer is reputed to have said that he was going to get not only the best ax that money could buy, but also a grindstone and a gasoline engine to turn it. Then he was going into a thicket and see how it felt to

---

[1] Boyce House, *Were You at Ranger?* (Dallas, 1935), p. 15.

attack a post oak with a really sharp ax.[2] Bob Duncan has a
version of the ax story from Beaumont.[3] Haldeen Braddy heard
it in Vann. George Sessions Perry must have heard it, for in one
of his short stories, he has a character say to another who had
oil land in East Texas, "He's got so much money he can't hardly
spend it. He bought three new axes an' a barrel of lamp oil an'
a barrel of flour, that didn't even make a dent in his money."[4]

Doubts therefore arise as to whether or not Mrs. McClesky
did in fact ask her husband for a new ax. She and her husband are
dead and their children have left the state. Among their neighbors the story is widely believed, but I have found no informant
who will vouch for its authenticity. Mrs. Hagerman, the widow
of the first mayor of Ranger, for example, said that since Mrs.
McClesky did not consider herself too good to go to the woodpile
and cut up an armful of wood, the story was not impossible. She
said, however, that many stories were told about the McCleskys
which she knew to be false. She said that at one time in the
Ranger-Breckenridge area "a McClesky" was used as a common
noun to designate any comic story of the newly rich.

John Rust, who lived on the farm adjoining the McCleskys
and was twelve years old when the well came in, said in a tape-
recorded interview:

> Yes, I heard the story and I've always doubted that it's true.
> It could be true certainly, and I'm not sitting here to say that
> it's not a true story.... I will tell you that I didn't hear her
> make the remark, but then of course she could have made it ...
> without my presence. But knowing her ... and her husband as
> I have known them for years, all my life, and the kind of peo-
> ple they are ..., I just don't believe that she made the remark
> at all. She might have made it, however, in a joking sort of way,

---

[2] Ibid., p. 78.
[3] Bob Duncan, *The Dicky Bird Was Singing* (New York, 1952), p. 268.
[4] George Sessions Perry, *Hackberry Cavalier* (New York, 1944), p. 42.

just for fun. But to seriously make the remark, I doubt if she would make it.

I know that they didn't do silly things with their money; they were good, thrifty people. They always had plenty to eat and they looked presentable in their clothes. Old John McClesky was the kind of man that didn't have his ax blade gapped up anyhow. He had an old-fashioned grindstone—I remember where it used to sit—and I've been over there before the oil boom at their home, and maybe old John would be gone somewhere or out in the field working or something, and Aunt Cordie would need some wood to cook the evening meal. I've gone out there and picked up that ax, and I remember that it always had a sharp blade.

And I just have every reason to kind of doubt that she made the remark.

Joe Weaver, retired oil operator who came to Texas from West Virginia by way of Oklahoma, and who was beginning operations in the Ranger area before the McClesky well came in, said that he did not believe the story. Then he said he would tell me what he called "an old West Virginia story." Oil was discovered on a widow's farm, "and her boys went to Harpersburg to celebrate. They had had a tough time and the widow had been a very hard worker. And the boys were enjoying themselves when one turned to the other saying, 'We must take Mother a gift,' and the other one said, 'Well, what in the world will we take her?' And the first suggested, 'I know, we will take her a new ax.' "

Tradition does not indicate that the first purchase of every suddenly enriched landowner was an ax. It might be a stalk of bananas, a cookstove, linoleum for the kitchen floor, a XXXX beaver Stetson. But the ax seems to be the most constant symbol of the new status. Its appeal may rest partly on irony. Oil brings a new fuel and makes the family chopping ax obsolete.

Another motif is that of the lucky breakdown. As drilling

equipment is being moved to a wildcat location made by a geologist, transportation fails and the well is drilled at the scene of the breakdown. It is a producer, but when the original location is later drilled, the well is a duster.

This story, observes Samuel W. Tait, Jr., "has been related about every oil field I know, whether it be sandy desert, boggy swamp, muddy prairie, or rocky mountain, and it has probably happened in every one of them."[5] The one instance that Tait vouches for happened in the sandy desert of California in 1895.

There are several occurrences of the story in Texas. Of these I have been able to verify only one, and it is little known. J. R. Webb of Albany, Texas, entered into a partnership with a relative to drill a well in Shackelford County, where oil, when found at all, was encountered at shallow depths. The partner, a geologist, now a man of high position in an oil company, made the location on the top of a hill. When machinery arrived it was found that the trucks could not be driven up the grade, and in those pre-bulldozer days the construction of a road involved more money that they cared to risk. They set up the rig at the base of the hill and got oil. Part of the returns from this well were used to build a road to the original location, where drilling brought a dry hole.

Few people have heard of the Webb-Crutchfield experience, but nearly everybody in Texas and Oklahoma knows the legend of the Fowler Farm Oil Company.

S. L. Fowler, owner of a large and rich cotton farm in the Red River valley just north of the little town of Burkburnett, Texas, in 1918 decided to give up farming and become a ranchman. He figured that the proceeds from the sale of his farm would buy sufficient grassland to sustain a herd large enough to make him a good living. The only difficulty was that Texas has a community property law, and Mrs. Fowler would not consent to the sale. She

---

[5] Samuel W. Tait, *The Wildcatters* (Princeton, 1946), p. 113.

was quoted by one journalist as saying: "I believe there's oil under our land, and I won't agree to dispose of the farm until a test is drilled. If oil isn't found, I'll sign the papers; but the people of this section have undergone so many hardships with such patience that I just know there is something good in store for them."[6]

Finding his spouse adamant, Fowler decided that the only way to sell the farm was to meet her condition, so he called on his neighbors for help. He figured that it would take $12,000 to put down a well deep enough to satisfy his wife. He put up a thousand dollars and his friends subscribed varying amounts until the sum was raised. One of the subscribers was Walter Cline, a drilling contractor who happened to have an idle rig in North Texas at the moment. In exchange for a thousand-dollar interest in the venture, he agreed to furnish the rig and the services of his drilling superintendent.

A geologist was employed, according to legend, who staked out a location in the cotton field. The wagon hauling the first load of equipment bogged down in the sand. "Oh well, unload her here," Fowler said, for for his purpose one place was as good as another.

The well came in and opened the Burkburnett Field. After a few months the Fowler Farm Oil Company sold out for $1,800,000, paying the shareholders $15,000 for each one hundred invested.

The figures are history and a part of the legend is true. Neighborliness did enter into the formation of the company. Sand had something to do with the location of the well, and a well drilled later north of the discovery produced only salt water. The rest is imagination.

As Walter Cline remembers, the project began to take shape one day in front of Luke Daley's drug store, "where we usually

---

[6] Boyce House, *Oil Boom* (Caldwell, 1941), p. 39.

congregated and did our whittling and settling really heavy problems."

S. L. [Fowler] broke the news to the bunch [Mr. Cline continues] that he wanted to dispose of his cotton land and get him a piece of ranch land but that his wife thought they ought to drill a well on the land and that he didn't have money enough and he was going to have to get some help, and he wanted to know if any of us would be interested. Well, there was nothing particularly favorable to encourage anyone to want to spend any money or time or effort on the Fowler land. On the other hand, there was nothing that definitely condemned it. So we sat around and decided that just as friends and neighbors, we'd just do our boy scout good turn by putting in a little, not enough to hurt any of us, but maybe enough to poorboy a well down. . . .

And we got enough money committed to look like we could afford to drill a well. The question of location then came up and we decided there wasn't any use in pulling a whole lot of sand, going way out in this cotton patch, and we'd drill it reasonably close to town. So we went right north of the hog pen that was east of S. L.'s house with a lane through there and a gate, drove out in the field where we had driven a stake and drilled there.

I'd like to interject here the statement that there's been very few discovery wells brought in that the myth hasn't started that they decided to drill a well on a given ranch or a given farm or on a given part of ground and they started out and it rained like the devil or they broke the wagon wheel or the truck broke down, and they were already on the property where they wanted to drill and they were a half-mile or a mile from the location, and they said, "Oh well, hell, let's just unload it. One place is as good as another. We're on the right land. We'll drill it here."

Well, now I heard that. I've heard it about the Fowler well and I've heard it about practically every discovery well that's been drilled in Texas in my time, and I have yet to find a single instance of where that's true. I just don't think there's a bit of truth in it. I know it's not true so far as the Fowler well is

concerned. We drilled the Fowler well right where we intended
to drill it, and right where we drove our stake. And that definitely settles the Fowler well.[7]

Another and more elaborate version of the lucky breakdown
story is the one concerning Santa Rita, the discovery well in the
Big Lake Field, the first of the oil fields to be opened on the
endowment lands of the University of Texas.

The earliest published version of this story that I have found
is that of Owen P. White in the *New York Times* for May 3,
1925.

> When the lease was signed Krupp [Hyman Krupp, organizer
> and president of the company] went to work. He hired ex-
> pensive oil experts . . . to go out and locate the proper anticlines
> for him and then after this had been done, busied himself in
> getting together enough money to drill the well. . . . The months
> flew by until the date on which the lease would automatically
> expire was dangerously near. Krupp redoubled his efforts and
> finally, with only a few days to go, he took the road with three
> trucks loaded with drilling equipment.
>
> When Krupp was still several miles away from the precious
> stake, which had cost him several thousand dollars to have
> driven in the ground, one of his trucks broke down completely,
> and—there he was! At that time, as the story goes, he had only
> two days left. What should he do? There was no possibility of
> being able to reach the desired destination with his outfit. The
> breakdown had occurred on land covered by his lease and so,
> with no high-salaried geologist at hand to advise him, but mere-
> ly because the ox was in the ditch and he had to act at once to
> prevent forfeiture, Krupp set up his rig at the scene of the dis-
> aster and went to work .

Another version of the tale was included in the general report
of the Sun Oil Company covering operations in West Texas and
New Mexico up to November 1, 1929. A paragraph reads:

[7] Tape-recorded interview, Wichita Falls, August 13, 1952 .

An unusual incident occurred when the Big Lake Field in Reagan County was discovered in 1923. Location for their first test was made some two miles westward, but owing to a breakdown while transporting the materials to the location, they unloaded just where the incident happened, and this well, while it led to a small producer, led to the discovery of the Big Lake Field. Had the first test been drilled where the location was originally made, possibly new chapters would have been written regarding the field. Subsequent tests have proven their first location would have been a failure.[8]

A writer in the *Daily Texan*, student newspaper of the University of Texas, for February 9, 1940, told the story as follows:

The site, in the southwestern part of Reagan County, at which the first oil well was completed in May, 1923, was chosen purely by accident. The drilling party, headed by Frank Pickrell, was bogged down. Since the lease was to expire in a few hours, members decided to drill where they were stranded.

They drilled not on their own lease, but on a part of the 2,000,000 acres provided by the Constitution for the University endowment fund and now known as the Big Lake Field.

But for a real professional handling of the story, we turn to the Austin *Statesman* for January 23, 1940.

The ragged country with its old worn jutting hills, crouched beneath the terrible drenching from the rains. Little rivers ran where dry gulches with their platted grasses formerly cut through the terrain.

In slicker and chewing the end of an old cigar, a man named Frank Pickrell peered from the switch house into a torrent of rain, walked impatiently back and forth.

"All right, boys," he said, "I've got a lot of money tied up in

[8] This and the two newspaper stories following are quoted by Martin Schwettmann, "The Discovery and Early Development of the Big Lake Oil Field," M.A. thesis, University of Texas, 1941.

this. We've got to take a chance. We've got to get this machinery going."

And the boys got up and in the heavy rain began loading the rig and drilling machinery on the cumbersome wagons. In a little while they got started.

Mud clawed at the wheels and sucked at the mules' feet. The animals grunted and strained at the traces and the wagons creaked through the slime over the treacherous roads.

"Just seven miles to go," encouraged Mr. Pickrell. The rain poured. The men cursed and cracked whips, and wiped the mud from their eyes.

The geologist had said that oil would be found on a certain spot. Mr. Pickrell was determined to reach that spot. Then the rain came down in torrents. It almost hid one team from another. West Texas had never seen it rain like that before.

Up front there was much cursing. Hazy figures floundered here and there. Mr. Pickrell stalked up front. The lead wagon was mired. There wasn't any use, the straining mules could not budge it.

"We'll have to wait," said Mr. Pickrell. The boys huddled together to wait. The skies were puffed and swollen with clouds, and the rain chattered along the gullies and around the wagons.

They waited all day. Mr. Pickrell knew his West Texas. "Boys," he said, "this thing'll keep up. Another day and we'll be here two weeks getting to that place. Unload her here. We'll dig our well right here."

Now the testimony gathered by Schwettman from Pickrell and other participants in the event is to the effect that (1) it was not raining when the equipment was being moved; on the contrary, the ranchers were complaining about a long dry spell, (2) horses rather than mules or trucks were used to draw the equipment, (3) there was no breakdown, (4) the well was located where the geologist had driven the stake.

Pickrell had previously certified that the well had been located at the stake driven by the geologist and that it was upon the recommendation of the geologist that the well had been drilled. Moreover, the breakdown story became an issue in a lawsuit in 1926. The court found the story false and so stated in its judgment.[9] This, however, did not dispose of the legend. Three of the four written versions I have quoted came after the decision, and folks in Texas still talk about the lucky breakdown that first brought oil to their university.

The third motif is that of the million-dollar drink. This is no Coal Oil Johnny episode in which a million dollars is spent; instead, a million dollars is gained, though not for the celebrant.

In one form of the story that celebrant is a geologist. He is called upon to make a hurried decision, when, unfortunately, he is too drunk to study his data. He makes a random mark on the map, and when he sobers up he realizes that it is not on the structure as he had plotted it. He remains silent, however, and hopes for the best. The best happens, and subsequent drilling on the location he would have made had he been sober results in a dry hole.[10]

In the more common form of the story, the big brass in a distant city decide to abandon a well. But the driller or someone in the chain of authority between him and the president of the company fails because of drunkenness to see the order carried out. Drilling continues a few hours longer and a million-dollar sand is tapped.

This tale is told of the McClesky well, but it has met with no wide credence in the Ranger area.

The classical Texas example, like that of the lucky breakdown, comes from the Big Lake Field and involves Frank Pickrell. In 1928 a deep test known as University 1-B was being put down with cable tools. At a depth of 8,245 feet the bailer hung, the sand line parted, a long and expensive fishing job ensued, and the company decided to abandon the well. The order was not

9 Ibid., p. 20.
10 Duncan, *The Dickey Bird Was Singing*, pp. 37ff.

carried out, and the discovery of a new producing horizon resulted.

The reason the order was not carried out, according to a widely circulated report that reached print in the *San Angelo Standard-Times* for May 28, 1933, was the million-dollar drink.

> Late in Nov. 1928 Frank Pickrell, Texon vice president, ordered a halt at 8,343 feet. The deep wildcat had cost over $100,-000. Cromwell reported that the formation looked promising and argued successfully that drilling continue. On Saturday, Dec. 1, the bit reached 8,518 in black lime. Pickrell again telephoned and this time insisted that work stop. Cromwell stopped to revive his spirits with what someone later aptly termed "a million dollar drink," and decided he could notify the crew the next morning. Meanwhile the drill kept pounding.
>
> Early the next morning the driller phoned Cromwell that the well was spraying oil. "Hit 'er another foot," Cromwell instructed and No. 1-B began to flow for a new world's record depth of 8,525 feet.[11]

Schwettman also investigated this legend. What basis it has in fact is indicated by a letter he received from Waldo Williams, chief driller.[12] Williams said that the "big boys had a meeting in New York and decided that $140,000 was enough to spend on a non-paying well." They ordered Pickrell to stop drilling at 8,500 feet. Pickrell then called Cromwell by telephone and gave the order. Cromwell then talked over the prospects of the well with Williams, and was so confident of success that he said instead of giving the order he would disappear for a few days. On the second day of December the well flowed forty barrels of oil.

Williams began trying to locate Cromwell. After two days, he was found at an editors' convention in Sweetwater. In a few hours after he received the message, he was on the location directing the completion of the well.

[11] Quoted by Schwettmann, "The Big Lake Oil Field," pp. 101-103.
[12] Ibid.

These are some of the local exemplifications of some of the motifs that seem to be coextensive with the oil industry in the United States. The tales have been only meagerly collected, and little can be said with assurance concerning the localities of their origin. Although I have not been able to verify any instances of the ax or the million-dollar drink stories, it is not improbable that they, like the legend of the lucky breakdown, have happened somewhere, perhaps more than once.

The stories I have dealt with and many others have been disseminated through both the spoken and the written word. The mobility of the personnel of the oil industry and the high rate of circulation of newspapers and magazines among the American people account for their wide diffusion. In no case have I been able to determine with certainty whether a local version was circulated first in oral or in written form. The newspaper account of Mrs. McClesky's ax followed so close upon the discovery of oil that my informants cannot say whether or not the tale had been previously in oral circulation. My belief is that the reporter had heard the story before and was the first to apply it to Mrs. McClesky.

The story of the lucky breakdown in connection with the Big Lake discovery was in oral circulation by midsummer following the completion of the well in May, 1923. The earliest version I have found in print is that of May 3, 1925. The earliest printed version of the million-dollar drink story that I know of was published May 28, 1933, nearly four and a half years after the event. The reporter intimated that the tale was then in oral circulation.

Whichever preceded, the history of these tales illustrates the manner in which the spoken and the printed word complement each other in the development of one type of folklore in a literate society.

Like most folk motifs, they involve the unusual, the unexpected. Yet why some stories are interesting and are widely repeated and others are not cannot be fully explained. But in any group there will be those who know a good story when they hear one and are not too strictly bound by facts to alter them if it makes the story better. And there will always be feature writers who are not averse to changing and embellishing facts to make salable copy.

8. On the Nature of Myth (1954)

The concept of myth has been greatly extended in our generation. It used to be assumed that myth-making was a characteristic of the primitive mind and was therefore confined to early stages of culture. But the more we have learned about the so-called primitive mind and the more we have learned about the sophisticated mind, the less they have seemed to differ. If human beings made myths in the past, it is safe to assume that they are making them in the present and will make them in the future.

The trend toward a general recognition of this assumption is evidenced by the increasing frequency with which the term "myth" is encountered in general reading. In the book review section of one issue of the *Nation*, for example, the word occurs in three separate reviews, not one of which is concerned with a

NOTE: Originally published in *Southwest Review* 39 (spring 1954): 131-136.

work specifically on mythology. In one we are warned against the danger that "brilliant nuances may be built up into a scientific mythology by the process of pyramiding quotations." In another, mention is made of the white collar class "celebrated in our mythology as the backbone of the nation," and in a third, myth is identified with an archetypical story, this one of incest.

The new *Dictionary of Folklore* defines myth in nineteenth-century terms, as "a story presented as having actually occurred in a previous age, explaining the cosmological and supernatural traditions of a people, their gods, heroes, cultural traits, religious beliefs, etc." In purport this corresponds to the primary definition in the second edition of the *New International Dictionary*.

Thus in one context it is implied that myth-making belongs to primitive culture, or at least to primitive groups within a culture, while in another context it is implied that myth-making continues in our own times, even among the scientists. Of course one may say that *myth* has different meanings in the two contexts, but if the myths of the past administered to the felt needs of human beings, I see no compelling reason for assuming that all these needs (except those of sex) are met by contemporary civilization. If myth functions in primitive cultures, it should also flourish in ours.

Trends toward a recognition of this thesis are discernible in certain anthropological writings of this century. Edmond Doutté's study of the culture of North Africa led him to define, in a work published in 1909, myth as "le désir collectif personnifié," and he assumed that primitive man resorted to myth and ritual because of his inability to reason, a judgment from which leading contemporary anthropologists dissent. Clyde Kluckhohn begins his "Myth and Ritual: A General Theory" by following Durkheim in defining myth as a "sacred tale," and in the course of his discussion refers to the mythology of Nazi Germany. He does not specify in what respect the Nazi mythology is made up of tales nor in what sense it is sacred. Nazi mythology is referred to also by Josef Rysan, who makes a distinction between religious myth, characteristic of the past, and social myth, typical of the present. Finally, there is Bronislaw Malinowski, who accepts the Durkheim definition of myth, but whose work is especially significant because of his insistence that myth must be studied in its social context and because of his suggestion that "the science of myth in living cultures, such as the present civilizations of India, Japan, China, and last but not least, our own, might well be inspired by the comparative study of primitive folklore," a study he has not yet undertaken.

These various meanings of myth may be synthesized and the diverse materials denominated myth may be unified under the general definition that a myth is a belief held by some cultural group about the relations between man and superhuman powers, whether these powers are conceived of as spirits or as impersonal forces—natural, economic, or what not. The belief must have social acceptance, though not necessarily of the dominant group. A belief held only by a single individual or several random individuals is not a myth. There is some cohesion in the group which is both cause and result of the acceptance of the myth. A myth is not necessarily false. It may exhibit any degree of probability short of certainty, which is possible only in extremely limited fields of discourse. The belief is held to be of social importance and to demand an appropriate pattern of behavior. It is sacred or religious not in the sense that it must be concerned with spirits and deities, but in the sense that it is held with a warm conviction and is associated with the most cherished values of the believers.

The more these values are threatened, the more vigorously will the myth be defended. When a myth is no longer believed, it ceases to be a social force and becomes literature of the past, an item of history.

If myth is to be defined in these terms, then it cannot be restricted to narrative forms. There is good reason, however, for calling the great archetypical stories, those on such themes as redemption, atonement, attempted flight from a god, incest, and the like, myths. They are often embodied in fiction and biography. But the specific narrative embodiment is not the myth per se, and it is possible to believe the myth without believing in the historicity of a single specific narrative embodiment of it. In content myths are descriptions of processes, accounts not merely of what has taken place, but of what now takes place and of what will take place in the future; the process is assumed to be timeless. Myths of racial superiority, for example, have been based on (1) special creation of the superior race, (2) a covenant entered into by an ancestor of the race and a god, (3) descent from supermen, or often demigods, (4) superior physical characteristics, (5) empirical evidence of superior achievement. In each case it is assumed that the superiority is permanent. There are myths in all realms of opinion where man is considered in relation to the world. And to these realms, as I. A. Richards has observed, belongs "everything about which civilized man cares most . . . ethics, metaphysics, morals, religion, aesthetics, and the discussions surrounding liberty, nationality, justice, love, truth, faith and knowledge."

This list of values, of course, is not intended to be complete. It omits entirely material things like food and shelter, values which myth also serves. The scholarship of mythology has in the main been too much concerned with theme and not enough with function, and such definitions of the psychological functions of myth as have been made have failed in being too specific, in explaining all myth in terms of one or a few specific motivations such as promotion of fertility in plants and animals, curiosity about the moon, or sexual desire. An examination of specific myths and analyses made of them point to two basic desires under which specific wants may be integrated. They are security and dignity. The relative emphasis on the one or the other will vary from culture to culture and from group to group within a culture.

Since man cannot feel secure in an utterly capricious world, the first assumption of the universal myth is that there is order in the universe, physical and moral. In primitive societies the world is conceived of in terms of personality. It is controlled by a person or more often by a plurality of persons, subject to much the same emotions that influence human behavior. Security is obtained by keeping these persons in a good humor, largely through prayer and ritual. In modern civilization increasing reliance is placed on impersonal forces, thought to be uniform in their operation.

Complete security would result from a power that automatically met all the needs of men. Yet no mythology presupposes such a condition on earth. Perhaps the empirical evidence is too strong. Suffering and death cannot be ignored. But important also is the loss of human dignity such an arrangement would entail. It would deny man any freedom and reduce all his acts to insignificance. Thus some element of uncertainty must remain. A second basic assumption, therefore, is that evil is a part of the world order. The devil is as important as the angels.

The universal myth further assumes that men and the institutions they create may choose between good and evil. The amount of human freedom varies with different mythologies, but even the most rigidly deterministic religions and philosophies hold men accountable for their acts. Another tenet in the universal myth is that while the good will ultimately triumph, if not here then in a future world, the choices men make here are of cosmic importance. Thus in the mythology of Social Darwinism the law of progress was irreversible, yet man had a veto power over it. By philanthropy and social legislation he could interfere with the operation of the immutable law.

Security, then, came in part from man's limited power to control natural and social phenomena. When the universe is conceived of as being governed by supernatural spirits, control is largely through ritual, in the narrow sense of the word, though even the most primitive people have a considerable body of practical knowledge. As knowledge advances, techniques of control become increasingly scientific. But control is never complete, so that one source of security is resignation, even destruction of the individual will. Paradoxically this may be also a source of dignity. The individual takes his importance from the world soul into which he is absorbed or from the master race of which he is a member.

Thus, as twentieth-century scholarship is unanimous in agreeing, myths arise from the deep needs of human beings. There is no such unanimity as to the relative importance of the individual and society in the creation of myths; and in the crude form in which the question is often put, it is meaningless. No individual inventor is likely to be found for the story of Prometheus or for the Navaho story of Spider Woman. The unity of the style often found in narratives may be that of the scribe or oral informant, and is not significant in the argument.

Many myths are associated with individual men. Thus the Ghost Dance cults of the North American Plains Indians that arose at the end of the nineteenth century were based on the dreams or revelations of known men. Among them was Jack Wilson (or Wovoka, to use his Paiute name) who, during an illness with a fever and an eclipse of the sun, had a revelation concerning the rejuvenation of the earth and the restoration of primeval happiness. He prescribed also a ceremonial which, along with the myth, was accepted by neighboring tribes. But this acceptance depended upon prevailing social conditions. The Indians had been deprived of their food supply, many were starving, and their old tribal life had disintegrated. An individual does not found a myth in an unfavorable climate of opinion. Another example may be taken from American history. Four years after Wovoka's revelation, Frederick Jackson Turner propounded his thesis about the significance of the Frontier in American history, and founded a school of history. But the Turner thesis, somewhat distorted, did not become a part of the American mythology until the political conservatives seized upon it as a weapon against the rising liberalism of the 1920s and 1930s.

Moreover, both Wovoka and Turner had predecessors. New mystic cults began appearing among the Plains Indians as early as 1800, and Turner had been in part anticipated by Samuel Adams Hammett, Woodrow Wilson, and Hamlin Garland, to mention only a few of his forerunners. Both men also had disciples, and the role of the disciple is important in elaborating the myth and expanding it into a mythology.

When Doutté defined myth as collective desire personified, he implied that personification was an essential part of the mythological process. And Henry Nash Smith uses myth and symbol "to designate larger or smaller units of the same kind of thing, namely an intellectual construction that fuses concept and emotion into an image." That myth and symbol should be thus equated is doubtful, but it should be observed that every myth will find its symbols and that some of the symbols will be personalities. Thus personification is the usual result of the popular acceptance of a belief; that is, of its becoming a myth. To take examples from our own culture, it is not merely that certain persons become mythological symbols: Boone and Carson of manifest destiny, Theodore Roosevelt of red-blooded and aggressive nationalism, Franklin Roosevelt of courage in the face of economic disaster, Eisenhower of fatherly solicitude for his bewildered children; it is that institutions and ideas—the Pentagon, the Kremlin, free enterprise, and creeping socialism—are talked about and written about as persons. They are endowed with wills and emotions, a way of thinking to which the United States Supreme Court once gave the highest judicial sanction when it declared that the Southern Pacific Railroad and all other corporations were persons within the meaning of the Fourteenth Amendment.

All students of primitive culture have noted a relation between myth and ritual. Where myth is thought of as sacred tales of gods and spirits and ritual as pageantry featured by masks, costumes, dancing, and the like, the ceremonial is often a dramatization of the myth. In such cases the question arises as to whether the myth was a later creation to reinforce the ritual or whether the myth resulted in the initiation of the ritual. Since Frazer's time ritual has been generally considered primary, both psychologically and temporally. Yet examples from primitive cultures can be pointed out where the ritual clearly comes after the myth. And it can be shown further that not all myths have their accompanying ritual. There is none, so far as I know, based on the Oedipus myth. There would seem to be no necessary connection then between myth and ceremonial when defined in these narrow terms.

But as I have tried to indicate, these terms are too narrow: in our analyses of complex living cultures we must extend the concept of myths to beliefs other than those about gods. We should also inquire into the contemporary meaning of ritual. It has long been recognized that ritualism is not confined to appeals to spirits. Anthropologists like Herskovits, for example, have not hesitated to speak of secular rites, though Hortense Powdermaker is clearly talking nonsense when she speaks of profits as rituals. A ritual is not a thing, not even a bank account, but it need not be concerned with supernatural beings.

Nor does it necessarily involve the paraphernalia of pageantry such as masks, robes, and musical instruments, though the wearing of badges, uniforms, and the like no doubt does enhance the emotion of the participants. Black shirts have played no insignificant role in recent history. Rituals do not always involve group activity. Even within the most restricted meaning of the term private ritual is practiced in all cultures. But the greater effectiveness of group activity has long been obvious. Hence the political debate in which each side solidifies its own position, hence the mass cheering at football games, and hence mass parades and ceremonies in which the individual will is submerged in the will of the mass.

An essential characteristic of ritualistic behavior is that it seeks to achieve a result, either upon outside events, upon the mental state of the subject, or upon both. The object may be to bring rain or to reconcile one to death. It may be to bring about political action or to reconcile within the subject the dichotomy of selfishness and good will toward his fellow-man, to gain cosmic approval of what one wants to do.

Ritualistic behavior is both repetitive and nonrational. It prescribes the pattern of behavior and relieves the individual of the responsibility of thought; the behavior springs from the attitudes fixed by the myth. Thus if I believe that America was made great by a collection of discrete individuals each pursuing his own selfish ends and if I believe that this process is still operative, I will not have to think to define my attitude toward welfare legislation.

Thus myth and behavior enforce each other. There is no final answer as to temporal or psychological primacy. The conservative character of myth has been emphasized in anthropological literature. Yet radicalism and revolt have their mythology too. Wovoka's myth foretold a world in which there would be plenty of buffalo and no white men. Since it looked toward the re-establishment of a vanished past, it was reactionary, but since it was a protest against Indian life as it existed in 1889, it was also revolutionary. *Social Statics*, published in 1850, laid the foundation for a complex mythology in defense of unregulated capitalism. It was a new mythology, but it justified old behavior. *The Communist Manifesto*, published in 1848, laid the foundation of a complex mythology in defense of socialism. It was a new mythology looking toward new patterns of behavior. These and other examples that could be adduced suggest that myths in defense of the status quo develop after the ritual, and that those which attack the status quo develop before the ritual.

Thus it would seem that as cultures pass from illiteracy to literacy, their myths retain their basic assumptions about the general nature of the universe—that it is ordered, yet both good and evil, and that human beings make choices; that some such assumptions are imposed upon man by his desire for security and dignity; that relatively less emphasis will be placed on spirits and more on human manipulation in attaining these goals, and hence sanctions are sought increasingly in natural law and decreasingly in appeals to spirits; but that the role of myth—that is, of socially approved belief which results in repetitive and nonrational behavior—is as important as ever; and that the forces generated by myth may in a free society be either conservative or revolutionary.

9. Folklore in a Literate Society (1958)

T here will, I predict, be readers, particularly among those who teach English composition to college freshmen and have made the frustrating discovery that Johnny can't read, who will maintain that this essay can have no reference to the United States. Yet that is the reference intended. For even though Johnny can't read as well as his teacher wishes, and even though Americans read fewer books than the British, the scripts they listen to have been written by somebody. Besides, nearly everybody reads something—if not the *Philadelphia Bulletin*, then the *Readers' Digest*, the *Wall Street Journal*, the Dell Comic books, or the Rexall Almanacs. But even if there is an American who reads nothing at all, he lives in a culture whose most important determinant is the written word.

NOTE: Originally published in *Madstones and Twisters*, pp. 45–51. Publications of the Texas Folklore Society, no. 28 (Dallas: SMU Press, 1958).

What happens in America, therefore, has a significant bearing on what happens to folklore in a literate society.

When you read, let us say, Louis Adamic's description of a peasant wedding in Yugoslavia, with its mock fight for possession of the bride, suggestive of a remote antiquity when marriages were made by capture, you say, "How quaint. This is folklore." What do you say when you read about the weddings reported in the society pages of your local newspaper? Here are a couple of examples:

> Given in marriage by her father, the bride wore a white crystal waltz length gown with inset eyelet crystalette panels and bouffant skirt. The shoulder length veil of illusion was held in place by pearlized orange blossoms. . . . Following the ceremony, a reception was held in the fellowship hall of the church. After a trip to Florida, the couple will live in ——.

> Given in marriage by her father, the bride wore a floor length dress of lace over taffeta designed with a basque bodice, brief sleeves and a tiered skirt. Her fingertip veil was attached to a cap of Chantilly lace reembroidered with pearls and sequins.
> [Honor attendants] wore waltz length dresses of seafoam green chiffon over taffeta and net with matching crown headpieces and carried baskets of majestic daisies and English ivy.

Are the American weddings any less folkish because the bride and her mother had the advice of Emily Post and Neiman-Marcus rather than, or in addition to, that of the village elders? At least the veil remains, though its antique function has long been forgotten.

Other questions arise. When a carpenter learns to frame a roof by serving an apprenticeship and receiving instruction by word of mouth from a man who has received his in the same way, you may call his art a folk craft, that is, a tradition that has been handed down orally. But suppose the carpenter has studied a book on roof framing? Or—what is often true these days—he has gone to school and can prove the Euclidean propositions upon which the craft is based?

I have read in collections of folklore descriptions of Czech beer parties in honor of a christening. But I have never found in what purported to be a collection of folklore a description of a publisher's cocktail party in honor of an author's latest book. Yet each follows a historically determined pattern; each is a custom of a group with a common body of tradition. This is not to say that the traditions are of equal duration, or that they have been transmitted in exactly the same way.

One effect of literacy is high specialization and another is nationalism. As a nation gets bigger, its people become increasingly divided into occupational and other groups. Folklore has been mainly concerned with certain of these groups, to the exclusion of others. It began in Europe as a study of "vulgar errors" or "popular antiquities," and even after Thoms proposed the term *folklore* in 1846 its content for the most part continued to be the social anthropology of European peasants, and later of "primitive" people of other continents. Thus arose the concepts of survival and arrested development.

Thus arose too the idea that a "folk" must be a primitive group isolated from the contaminating influence of modern civilization. Mary Austin, for example, was able to find only three folk groups in the United States: the Red Indians, the Southern Negroes, and the Southern Mountaineers. These are all isolated geographically or socially or both. But there are other kinds of isolation, and there are many groups within the mass. An occupation, for example, unites its members, and at the same time partially separates them from the mass. Each occupation has its lore—partly belief, partly custom, partly skills—expressed in anecdotes, sagas, tales, and the like. Each individual in a literate society plays a multiplicity of roles, belonging as he does to more than one group. Take for example the railroad conductor who is also a baseball fan. He has a body of tradition appropriate to each role. He knows how to behave in each role, and he knows the verbal lore of each. He knows the witticisms that pass between conductors and passengers. He can tell you apocryphal tales about Jay Gould and Collis Huntington; he knows about Casey Jones and the slow train through Arkansas. He knows too about Casey at the bat, and has at his command all the formulas for heckling the other team and the umpire. Our culture is the richer for this pluralism.

Yet the mass in the United States may, I think, be properly referred to as a folk. For in spite of divisive influences of specialization, of geography, of race, the American people have more in common than in diversity. Charles Wilson and Walter Reuther are divided by class interest. Wilson believes that what is good for General Motors is good for the United States. Reuther believes that what is good for labor is good for the United States. One believes in the trickle-down theory of prosperity; the other in the seep-up theory of prosperity. But they both believe in prosperity. They speak the same language, have much the same concept of the mission and destiny of America, and neither is a conscious enemy of capitalism. One cannot assert that there is any one belief that every American accepts, but the presence of dissent does not prove the absence of a common body of tradition.

Even in a preliterate society tradition is never wholly static. One consequence of literacy is an acceleration of change. Learning develops not only new techniques but new values as well. As long as the American Negro saw no prospect of sharing in the white man's rising standard of living, his folklore concerned the values available to him. Charms took the place of the medical service he could not afford; superstition took the place of the education that was denied him. He consoled himself with tales covertly satirical of the white man and with the hope of justice when he crossed the River Jordan and was gathered to Abraham's bosom. Once convinced of the possibility of sharing in the good things about him, however, he announces without regret that Uncle Tom is dead—but not Uncle Tom's music, which he will cite with justifiable pride as a major contribution to American culture. This shift in emphasis is illustrative of one change folklore undergoes in a literate society.

Another change involves the crafts. The first effect of the industrial revolution is to drive out the folk crafts. Blankets from New England mills take the place of homemade quilts. Brussels and Axminster carpets appear on floors once covered by hooked rugs and rag carpets. Furniture comes from Grand Rapids rather than from the shop of the local cabinetmaker. In time, however, certain countervailing influences assert themselves. There is a revolt against the monotony of both the mass-produced article and the routine job by which most Americans earn their living; and as the shorter work week, the expansion of the service industries, and the availability of household appliances create leisure, and often boredom, people take up hobbies, and hobbies germinate new industries serving them. Markets are found for textile mill-ends, and the Rose of Sharon and the Wedding Ring begin to appear on beds; department stores display yarn and burlap, and hooked rugs reappear. The makers of power tools put on do-it-yourself campaigns, and men begin turning out coffee tables and four-posters in their basements. Most of the craftsmen will work from patterns furnished by their suppliers or the hobby magazine, but a few will create their own designs.

New crafts appear. Teen-aged boys learn that by doing certain things to their motors they can increase the noise, if not the power, of their jalopies. When this activity spreads over the country, somebody realizes that here is a clientele for a new magazine and *Hot Rod* appears on the newsstands. Then machine shops begin making the parts and selling kits to noncraftsmen, who, if they can afford to, may have their mechanics install them.

Even so, for the first time since the Stone Age great masses of

people have opportunity to give play to the instinct of workman-
ship, to find relief from the monotony of their jobs, and in some
degree to express whatever individuality they are endowed with.

As has been suggested by reference to the wedding veil, not all
old customs perish. In a culture dedicated as ours is to a continu-
ously rising standard of material well-being, a custom is likely
to survive, though with a changed significance, if its observance
increases the sales of goods and services. Readers of Keats know
that at one time a girl could, by performing certain rites on the
Eve of St. Agnes, see a vision of her future husband. The rites are
no longer performed. They required no purchasable equipment.
Not so with the suitable observance of Christmas, Thanksgiving,
Easter—and now Halloween, for of late we bribe the tricksters
with store-bought candy. We invent Mother's Day and Father's
Day, spacing them carefully so they will not come too close to
other already established occasions for spending money.

The pageantry that used to be associated with other occasions
—the tournament for example—will be adapted to the publicizing of local products. The Queen of Love and Beauty becomes
the Queen of Goats:

FREDERICKSBURG [Texas], July 25 (CTS)—A beautiful queen,
as much at home in ranching jeans as in regal robes that denote
her reign over the Mohair Realm, will officiate at the 38th annual coronation, show and sale of the Texas Angora Goat
Raisers' Association here Aug. 1, 2, and 3.

Her Mohair Majesty, we learn, will have the title of "Angora
Queen of the Universe," will be attended by "a score of attractive
duchesses," and will receive the homage of the queen of the
South Texas Fairs and Fat Stock Shows, the queen of the Gilles-
pie County Fair, and the Farm Bureau queen.

In a literate society verbal folklore will be disseminated not
only by loggers, cotton pickers, oil field workers, and traveling

salesmen, but also by historians, biographers, fictionists, and journalists, not to say folklorists. Songs, tales, proverbs will be published and read and some of them put into a wider oral circulation. In this process narrative lore, in particular, will undergo change. In the 1920s the journalists discover Paul Bunyan, who by this time is not only a logger but also an oil field worker, and begin writing about him for the general magazines. In order to make their material go as far as possible, they invent some tales and rewrite others long in the oral tradition, including many that have no connection with either logging or oil field work. In the meantime the loggers and oil field workers have become skilled manipulators of machines—power saws, power loaders, tractors, rotary rigs, and the like—and have lost interest in Bunyan. He becomes a national rather than a local or occupational folk character, standing for little more than bigness and strength. As Richard Dorson has observed, the journalists take him from the folk and give him back to a larger folk, but with a changed character and significance. And this will be true of any hero who attains more than local fame. Without the aid of writers he cannot move out of the province in which he has been created. The writers in moving him out must remold him into a type intelligible to the larger audience. Thus bad men become Robin Hoods, cowboys become knights-errant, backwoods politicians become symbols of militant democracy, lowly animals become symbols of lowly folk. Incidents are reported and transferred from one region to another. The journalists who covered the first oil boom, for example, garnered a considerable sheaf of rags-to-riches stories. Later journalists reported the same stories from other fields, and often in good faith, for the stories appear sometimes to have come from Pennsylvania to Texas first by word of mouth.

This essay will have achieved its purpose if it has raised more questions than it has answered. It has been written on the assumption that the processes which create folklore do not cease when a society becomes literate, and that the folklore of any culture will reflect the values of that culture. If it has demonstrated anything, it is that the oral and written traditions are not most fruitfully conceived as separate and distinct. Each is continually borrowing from the other as the processes of adaptation and creation continue.

10. The Family Saga as a Form of Folklore (1958)

It is with some hesitancy that I apply the term "family saga" to the subject of this paper. I am not here concerned with the heroic poems of Ireland or Iceland or the North European continent, dealing with battles and trials of strength and the complex genealogies of heroes. Nor may the narratives with which I am concerned be accurately called American analogues to these European works. I use the term mainly to denote a lore that tends to cluster around families, or often the patriarchs or matriarchs of families, which is preserved and modified by oral transmission, and which is believed to be true. Lore that is handed down *as* folklore is excluded. I am, then, not concerned with a type of tale, but with clusters of types, not with a motif, but with many motifs.

These clusters never form a connected history. Such a coher-

NOTE: Originally published in *The Family Saga and Other Phases of American Folklore*, pp. 1–19 (Urbana: University of Illinois Press, 1958).

ent narrative requires research in libraries and archives.[1] A history or biography written wholly or largely from oral sources has its values, but they are not the values of history or biography. What Homer Croy learned from the neighbors of Jesse James was folklore, a part of the James family saga.[2]

A consideration of these clusters of lore raises a number of questions, for which I have no final answers: What forms and motifs make up the family saga? What is their relation to history? What kinds of historical incidents survive in the oral tradition with little change? How do incidents, some historical and some folk tales of great antiquity, become incorporated into the family saga?

First, the general observation may be made that each episode has, in Martha Beckwith's phrase, "taken on, through . . . repetition and variation, the character of a group composition," and that it "functions in the emotional life of the folk."[3] For a tale to enter the oral tradition and survive, it must afford emotional satisfaction to the hearers, who then repeat the tale and thus widen its circulation. Nothing could be duller and, even when a product of the imagination, further removed from folklore than inventories of property and lists of offices of honor and trust held by one's ancestors.

An event in the family saga has a relation to a social context and reflects a social value. This does not mean, however, that the event is invariably in harmony with the actual social conditions of the region where it is believed to have happened. Two examples will illustrate this lack of harmony.

In one Texas family it is believed that an ancestress, during

---

[1] From the number of genealogists who clutter up the Barker Texas History Center, where I sometimes work, I estimate that a million people are at work on such histories.

[2] Homer Croy, *Jesse James Was My Neighbor* (New York, 1947).

[3] Martha Warren Beckwith, *Folklore in America*, Publications of the Folklore Foundation, no. 11 (Poughkeepsie, 1930), p. 3.

the Civil War, seeing a group of Union soldiers approaching the farm, began hiding the things of most value. Her most valued possession was a jewel box and its contents of diamonds, rubies, emeralds, and pearls. It developed that her fears were unfounded, for the soldiers were looking only for food, and when they had obtained it they left, and the mother and children began restoring the hidden articles to their proper places. But for some reason the jewel box was left in hiding. A few days later the mother died very suddenly, and the box, in spite of long and repeated searches, has never been found.

Now since Texas, where the family lived, was never invaded by Union soldiers, either the time or place is wrong. It could be that the troops were those of the occupation after the war; it could be that the story was transferred from the deep South, where the accepted thing was for the mistress of the plantation to bury the silver and jewels or have them carried off by the Yankees. If you wish, you may say that here is an etiological tale explaining the absence of family jewels.

In Massachusetts the accepted thing is for your ancestors to have been abolitionists associated with the underground railroad. Nathaniel Benchley, in a biography of Robert Benchley, writes of the first Benchley "to attract attention in Worcester" that after a political career, first as state senator and then as Lieutenant Governor, he, "feeling that the slavery problem needed more attention that he could give it from the Statehouse . . . went to Texas and set up a station on the underground railroad, helping slaves escape to the North. He was caught, convicted, and spent the rest of the time until Appomattox in a Texas jail."[4]

All this seemed rather strange to a certain Texas historian, Andrew Forest Muir. In the first place there was no reason for helping Texas slaves escape to the North, when Mexico, which welcomed Negroes and granted them full equality, was many

[4] Nathaniel Benchley, *Robert Benchley: A Biography* (New York, 1955), p. 21.

times nearer than Canada. Muir looked into the records and established that Henry W. Benchley was in Texas as early as April 12, 1859; that he taught singing lessons first in San Antonio and then in Houston; that after the Confederate Congress had passed an act exempting railroad employees from military service, he was a conductor on the Houston and Texas Central Railroad; and that on one occasion he got up a musical entertainment for Confederate troops. He never went to jail in Texas, and the railroad with which he was connected ran upon a flat coastal plain where not even a single tunnel was required.[5]

The tale clearly originated in Massachusetts in conformity with a pattern of conduct people of that state expect of their ancestors. It does not conform to a long tradition about why people came to Texas.

Long before Texas was a subject of concern to the people of the United States, it was assumed by the conservative well-to-do that anybody who left for the frontier did so for a good but hardly laudable reason.[6] Timothy Dwight thought that the people leaving New England must be a sorry lot, and Virginians used to say of one who left that state that he had gone to Hell or Kentucky. When people from the United States began moving into Texas and the political implications of foreseen annexation became apparent, the tradition that the frontiersman was a fugitive became intensified and localized. Thus a sort of archetype was created, which the Texans did little to refute. Samuel Adams Hammett, who was in Texas from 1835 to 1847, after writing a defense of the settlers, remarked that they were partly to blame for "the contumely heaped upon them. [They] indulged in a sly

---

[5] Andrew Forest Muir, "The Skeleton in Robert Benchley's Closet," *Southwest Review* 43 (winter 1958):70–72. To point out the inaccuracy of the story is not to convict Nathaniel Benchley of anything more serious than failure to verify what he set down as fact.

[6] Mody C. Boatright, *Folk Laughter on the American Frontier* (New York, 1949), pp. 1–15.

chuckle over their somewhat dubious reputation, and it was a
common joke to ask a man what his name at home was and what
he came to Texas for."[7] And according to W. B. Dewees, an early
Texas settler, the answer would be, "for some crime or other
which they had committed . . . if they deny having committed
any crime, and say they did not run away, they are generally
looked upon rather suspiciously. Those who come into the country at the present time [1831] frequently tell us rough, ragged,
old settlers . . . that they have a great deal of wealth in the States,
which they are going after as soon as they find a situation to suit
them. But we not relishing this would-be aristocracy generally
manage to play a good joke on them in return."[8] One day when
a number of these would-be aristocrats were boasting of their
"lands and Negroes and their ships at sea," they were thus addressed by "Old Man Macfarlane":

> "Well, gentlemen," he said, "I too once commenced telling
> that I had left a large property in the States, and in fact, gentle-
> men, I told the story so often that at length I really believed it
> true, and eventually started to go for it. Well, I travelled on
> very happily till I reached the Sabine River. . . . On its banks I
> paused, and now for the first time began to ask myself, What am
> I doing! Why am I here! I have no property in the States, and if
> I did, if I cross the river 'tis at the risk of my life, for I was
> obliged to flee to this country to escape punishment of the laws.
> I had better return and live in safety as I have done. I did so,
> gentlemen, and since that time have been contented without
> telling of the wealth I left in the States."[9]

The boasters were so angry that they would have injured the old
man had his friends not intervened, but this "put a stop to their
long yarns."

[7] Samuel Adams Hammett, *A Stray Yankee in Texas*, second edition (New
York, 1858), p. 4.
[8] W. B. Dewees, *Letters from an Early Texas Settler*, compiled by Clara
Corlelle, second edition (Louisville, 1853), p. 135.
[9] Ibid.

This attitude of the early settlers has persisted among their descendants, and many a Texas family saga begins with a G.T.T. —gone to Texas—story. That of Dandy Jim Smith will serve as an example.

In 1846, when Dandy Jim was a youth in Tennessee, there were in the community in which he lived two factions: the Mountain Boys and the Valley Boys, or the hill boys and the plantation boys. They crashed each other's parties and dances and had numerous fist fights. Then the Valley Boys brought knives into action, and the arms race was on. The Mountain Boys went to a Valley Boys' dance on a river boat with hickory clubs concealed in their pantlegs. The fight began on signal. A Valley Boy drew a pistol and shot a Mountain Boy in the knee. But the clubs were more effective than the single pistol, and many a Valley Boy was knocked off into the river. Some climbed back in their wet clothes and re-entered the fight, but when it was over, thirteen were missing. A mob formed and began rounding up the Mountain Boys. But not Jim and his brother Watt. They hid in a cave, where an old fisherwoman brought them food. They eventually got to Texas after shooting two of their pursuers.

I do not know that "Old Man Macfarlane" ever committed a crime in his life, nor do I know why Dandy Jim Smith came to Texas. I have told the story as I have had it from his descendants.[10] and I shall not offend them by trying to refute it.

Its significance in this context does not depend upon its accuracy as a biographical event. It is one example of the continuation of a long tradition with many variants. Sometimes it is the over-successful duelist who flees. Sometimes two men fight on a bridge; one is knocked into the river and drowns, the other goes to Texas. But the deed, whatever it is, must not indicate a crim-

[10] Angelina Smith, "Dandy Jim Smith," unpublished manuscript. This is largely a collection of tales gathered by Floyd Smith from "various relatives and old-timers," that is to say, from oral sources.

inal mind. It must not be robbery, embezzlement, or murder with malice aforethought. If any of these were the real crime, then the family saga would have to make a substitution or remain silent.

The saga of a pioneer family, as would be expected, will include adventures with wild animals. Because the frontiersman was armed with a superior rifle, and because he had been sufficiently touched by the Enlightenment to look upon the animals as natural creatures that could be killed with powder and lead, these adventures rarely exhibit the superstitious fear characteristic of the older Indo-European folklore. The typical hunt had little in it to catch the popular fancy. As Jim Doggett put it, "It is told in two sentences—a bar is started, and he is killed. The thing is somewhat monotonous."[11] Stories that pass into the oral tradition are likely to reveal (1) the uncommon sagacity of the hunter or (2) show human beings in jeopardy.

The first is exemplified by a story of how Adam Lawrence[12] relieved the starving colony. It was a time of prolonged drought and all the game had left the country, though crows occasionally flew over. Lawrence shot one to learn what it had been eating, and found an acorn in its craw. He knew there "was plenty of fat game where that crow drew his rations." He led a party in the direction the crows had come from, and after traveling many miles, they found oak trees and fat buffalo, bear, deer, and elk.[13]

For a story placing a human being in jeopardy, the panther was the favored animal. He, of course, was not a man-hunter,

---

[11] T. B. Thorpe, "The Big Bear of Arkansas," in *Tall Tales of the Southwest*, edited by Franklin J. Meine (New York, 1930), p. 16.

[12] Adam Lawrence came to the Red River Valley in 1815 and joined Austin's colony in 1822. Stories about his adventures were written, some in the first person, by W. S. Wade, before Lawrence's death in 1878. A typescript of Wade's work, entitled "Tales of Early Texas," has been furnished me by John Poindexter Landers, a great-grandson of Lawrence.

[13] The elk were evidently thrown in for good measure. They are not native to Texas.

and it was said that a man could take a willow switch and a feist dog and drive him out of the country. But he would fight when cornered, he might be attracted by the smell of fresh meat, and he sometimes attacked men, or apparently more often women, on horseback, perhaps in search of horsemeat, of which he was fond. There are recorded instances of his having killed children, and he was thought to regard a nursing baby as an especial delicacy.

I shall call the two panther themes occurring with greatest frequency "The Panther on the Roof" and "The Panther in Pursuit."[14]

My example of the first is from the Glimp family saga.[15] The Glimp family went on a bear hunt to lay in a supply of meat for winter, Sarah and her three-month-old baby along with the menfolks. Near where they expected to find bear, they built a log hut with a fireplace and clay-daubed chimney. They laid a roof of unspecified material on pole rafters. The men cut and brought in a supply of firewood, and left Sarah with her baby and a hound while they went to look for bear.

During the afternoon the baby began crying from colic. At dusk it was still crying. As Sarah got up to close the door, she heard a panther scream. He screamed three times, each time sounding nearer. Then she heard him near the door, his snarls answered by the growls and barks of the dog. The next sound she heard was the thud of the panther's landing on the roof, which sagged under his weight as he walked. The baby cried and the dog barked. The panther walked toward the chimney. She knew it was large enough for him to come through. She started piling wood on the fire, and kept piling it on until she noticed

[14] Two versions of the "The Panther on the Roof" and five versions of "The Panther in Pursuit" may be found in J. Frank Dobie, *Tales of Old Time Texas* (Boston, 1955), pp. 181–194.

[15] J. D. Brantley, "Reminiscences of a Texas Pioneer," unpublished manuscript.

that the clay was cracking. If it fell and exposed the sticks, the cabin would burn down. Her problem was to keep just the right amount of heat going up the chimney. Eventually the baby went to sleep. She put him on a pallet and seated herself by the fire with a knife in her hand. She was still sitting there awake when then men returned next morning.

With the dog they soon found the panther not more than a hundred yards away, and shot it. Although the hound was well trained and had always been obedient, he leaped upon the panther as it fell from the tree and could not be called away until he had completely ruined the hide.[16]

The motif of the panther in pursuit is essentially that of the fairy tale in which the hero, pursued by an ogre, drops objects which become obstacles to slow down the pursuer. The objects, however, are not bottles of water that become great lakes or twigs that become dense forests.

When J. Frank Dobie was a boy he used to hear a neighbor tell of a turkey hunt he once had. Taking his shotgun, for which he discovered he had only two loads, he got on his horse late one afternoon and rode toward a turkey roost. About a half-mile from the roost he came to a fence. There he tied his horse and walked on. He hid and waited for the turkeys to settle down and for the moon to rise. In the moonlight he aimed at several turkeys lined up on a limb and fired both barrels. Six turkeys fell. He was carrying them toward his horse when he heard a panther scream right behind him. He dropped one of the turkeys and ran as fast as he could. He had not gone far when the panther screamed again. He dropped another turkey. He dropped the last one just in time to leap on his plunging horse as the panther screamed again.

Dobie used to wonder what would have happened if the man

---

[16] On whether the event happened before or after the family moved from Tennessee to Texas in 1822, Sarah Glimp's descendants are not agreed.

had killed only five turkeys or if his horse had been a mile away instead of a half-mile. It was not till years later that he learned that the story had been "told for generations in many localities, pieces of venison or other game sometimes substituting for the dropped turkeys."[17]

Sometimes the substitute is articles of clothing, and the person in flight is a woman with or without a baby. She is riding in a vehicle or on horseback, when a panther screams and gives chase. Purposely or accidentally she drops her scarf or the baby's cap. The panther, attracted by the human scent, stops and smells and nuzzles the article of clothing, giving the woman a chance to get ahead. But he is soon coming again faster than the fastest horse can run. She drops another garment. She may strip the baby before she gets home, but no version has come to my attention in which she had to twitch her own last garment off.

Again, as would be expected, the pioneer family saga reflects the conflicts with the Indians, but here again it is selective. An Indian attack on a settlement or a party of hunters, where little happens except that men on both sides get killed, survives as an item of history. It survives in documents and books, but not in the folk memory. The event will pass into the oral tradition only when there is some added interest.

Sometimes this interest is comic, as in the story of the slow mule. The version that follows is from the Adam Lawrence saga. As Wade had the story, the Indians stole nearly all the horses in the settlement, and Lawrence organized a mustang hunt to replace them. Soon after the party had made camp the first night, a man named Jim Jones rode up on a long-legged mule and begged to join them. Lawrence told him that that would be impossible, for they were going into Indian country and might have to run for their lives. "If that happened," he said, "the Indians would sure catch you on that mule and scalp you."

[17] Dobie, *Tales of Old Time Texas*, pp. 183–184.

Jones insisted, however, and was finally permitted to go at his own risk. One day when he and Lawrence were scouting for mustangs some distance from the camp, where pens had been built, they topped a hill and saw about forty Comanches in war paint and feathers not more than six hundred yards away, coming toward them. The Indians raised a war whoop and charged. The two white men made a run for camp. They kept well ahead of the Indians for three or four miles. Then the mule began to "throw up his tail." Lawrence begged Jones to leave the mule and get up behind him, but Jones refused, saying the horse could not carry two men and both would be killed. He gave his watch to Lawrence, asking him to send it to his mother and tell her that nobody was to blame but him. This seemed final and there was no time for further parley. Lawrence rode on.

Two or three minutes afterwards [Wade has him say] I heard an awful screeching and yelling, and my heart came in my mouth, for I thought they was scalping Jim. But they weren't, for just then I heard a pat, pat right behind me, and I whirled back with my rifle gun cocked, for I thought it was an Indian; but I saw it was Jim, and you ought to have seen that mule, as it passed by me almost like I was standing still. Its nose was sticking straight out and smoke was a-coming out of it like steam out of a kettle. Its ears was laid back on its neck like they was pinned back. Its tail was a-sticking out behind him and it looked like he was jumping forty feet at a time. I noticed three arrows sticking up in that mule's rump. As Jim passed me he hollered back and said, "Farewell, Ad." What was them Indians yelling about? Why they was watching that mule fly. They turned back north.

When I got to camp the boys were behind trees with their guns ready, but I told them that them Indians wouldn't follow us in the timber, for they knowed when we shot we got meat. Jim had his saddle off trying to pull the arrows out of his mule. I roped his fore feet and throwed it and cut them out. I was a little careless when I let it up, for it made a bulge and away it went, looking back to where it had been introduced to the Indians. We never saw hide or hair of it again.[18]

The story of the scalping of Josiah Wilbarger, as will be apparent, is a complex one, combining a number of motifs. In August, 1833, Wilbarger was with a surveying party near where the city of Austin is now. At that time the only settlers in the region were Reuben Hornsby and his family and retainers. Six miles from Hornsby's house the surveyors were attacked in camp by Indians. Two men were mortally wounded. One after another Wilbarger's legs were pierced by arrows. The two unwounded men ran for their horses, Wilbarger following after them as best he could. They had mounted when they saw him fall, shot in the back of the neck with a gun. They left him for dead and rode full speed to Hornsby's.

Wilbarger did not lose consciousness, but he knew that his chances of staying alive depended upon his playing dead. This he did successfully, even while the Indians stripped him of all his clothing but one sock, and scalped him. When the scalp was torn from his head, he experienced no sharp pain, but heard a loud noise like thunder.

Then he lost consciousness. When he regained it he was alone. He dragged himself to the creek, rolled into the water and drank and rested. Becoming chilled, he crawled out and lay in the sun. Later he went back to the creek, drank, ate some snails, and began crawling in the direction of the Hornsby cabins. Exhausted, he lay down with his head against a tree.

As he lay there, a form. which he recognized as that of his sister, Margaret Clifton, who lived in Missouri, appeared and

[18] On Lawrence, see note 12. John Duval has a version of this story in *The Young Explorers*, first published serially in 1870–1871, and in *Early Times in Texas* (Austin, 1892), pp. 150–154. His principal characters are Uncle Seth and Bill Shanks, rather than Lawrence and Jones, and his mule is not hit by the Indians' arrows.

said, "Brother Josiah, you are too weak to go by yourself. Remain here, and friends will come and take care of you before the setting of the sun." When she had said this she moved away in the direction of the Hornsby place.

The men who had escaped reported Wilbarger dead. They had seen him fall with fifty Indians swarming around him. That night Mrs. Hornsby woke from a dream, called her husband and told him that Wilbarger was still alive. In her dream she had seen him wounded, naked, and scalped, but alive. Reuben Hornsby, thinking that his wife's nerves had been overwrought by the events of the day, calmed her and told her to go back to sleep. She did, only to be awakened by the same dream, the image of Wilbarger by the tree.

This time she got up, made coffee, and would not let the men rest until they promised to go to Wilbarger's relief at daybreak.

At the time of his rescue Wilbarger told of the apparition of his sister. Mails were slow in those days, and it was not until a month later that he got a letter from Missouri bringing the news of his sister's death on the day before he was wounded. He lived eleven years longer and his descendants still tell his story without significant variation.[19] A text has been in print since 1889,[20] which no doubt has militated against change. Yet one wonders how as a folk tale it could be improved.

The first chronicler, puzzled by the event he had recounted, concluded: "We leave to those more learned the task of explaining the visions of Wilbarger and Mrs. Hornsby. It must remain a marvel and a mystery."[21]

---

[19] The story as told by Wilbur C. Gilbert, a grandson of Josiah Wilbarger, was tape recorded July 23, 1953. Gilbert mislocates the Hornsby ranch by about twenty miles, a fact that would indicate that he had not recently read the published version.

[20] J. W. Wilbarger, *Indian Depredations in Texas* (Austin, 1889), pp. 2–13.

[21] Gilbert, see note 19.

There is no marvel or mystery in the incredible. In most segments of our population the ghost story survives only as a quaint relic of the past. It will not be a part of the living folklore unless it is both marvelous and believable. The Wilbarger story passes this test, as do a few others. A college student has recently written:

> When the writer's great-grandmother was a young girl in her early teens, she attended a slumber party given by one of the neighbors, at which about ten girls were present. Even in those days none of the guests slept at a slumber party. As the night wore on, the conversation turned to ghosts, ghost stories, and cemeteries. All but one girl admitted they would be afraid to go to a cemetery at night. The one girl held fast to her boast that she was afraid of nothing, not even ghosts. The other girls called her bluff and double-dared her to go to the Liberty Grove cemetery, which was about a mile and a half away. She took the dare; and to prove that she had fulfilled her mission, she was to take a knife and stick it in the grave of a person they all knew who had recently passed on. She took the knife and slipped out of the house.
>
> Next morning she was found stretched across the grave, her face frozen in an expression of terror. The hem of her skirt was pinned to the grave by the knife.[22]

The old dream-book lore seems to be gone. People who dream of a death no longer expect a wedding, and people who dream of muddy water no longer expect a death. Nor has a Freudian symbolism supplanted the old. Dreams that get into the family sagas are, like Mrs. Hornsby's, direct and obvious in their meaning.

A recent example concerns the Rust family, formerly of Ranger. As John Rust tells the story after hearing it from his parents "a countless number of times," his mother awoke one morning

[22] Maurita Russell Lueg, "Russell Tales," unpublished manuscript.

and said, "Jim, we'll never sell this little farm. Regardless of what happens, we'll hold on to it as long as we live."

He said, "Why, Mary, do you feel that way about it all of a sudden?"

She said, "Last night I had a dream. Look out this kitchen window, up here at this side of the hill, will you, just a hundred feet away? See that old live-oak tree out there, the largest tree on our place?"

He said, "Yes, what about it?"

"Well, right there under that tree is where we will find our fortune, because in my dream last night it was very vivid—the picture of that tree—and our fortune will be found right there under that tree. Now in what form my dream did not let me know, but I know . . . that that dream was more than a dream —it was a vision."[23]

In 1915 a neighbor of the Rusts named Jim Baker, "who had become famous in that section of the country for locating water wells with a peach-tree limb," came to the Rust home and said he had always had a feeling that there was silver upon the hill, and asked permission to prospect there. Jim Rust told him to go ahead—he could have half of all the silver he found. Baker cut a fork from a peach tree, tied a dime to it and began walking over the farm. The peach fork turned down and came to rest under the tree of Mrs. Rust's dream. Baker showed up the next day with an auger and began boring by hand. At about a hundred feet, however, he gave up hope and quit.

Two years later oil was discovered on the adjoining McClesky farm, and the Texas and Pacific Coal and Oil Company leased the Rust farm. Two days later workmen came and cut down the big live oak in order to make room for the drilling rig. The well came in, making ten thousand barrels a day.

"I guess there might be something in dreams," concludes John

23 From a tape-recorded interview with John Rust, Borger, Texas, September 15, 1952.

Rust. "There was something in that dream. The fortune was there just like the dream told my mother years before."[24]

There can be found in Texas, however, a considerable number of families whose total wealth is less than a million dollars. Of these a considerable number sometime in the past have barely missed getting rich. If it was in this century, the fortune would have been made in oil. Father or grandfather had a farm or a ranch or some timberland a mile or two or three from a newly introduced wildcat well producing X thousand barrels of oil a day. Various producers wanted to lease his land. They bid the price up to X thousand dollars an acre. But father or grandfather held out for more. In the meantime a well was going down between the discovery well and his land. It was dry.

Or, a small independent wildcatter was poorboying a well. At fifteen hundred feet his last dollar was gone. He went to father or grandfather and offered him a large interest in the venture for enough cash to drill another five hundred feet. Father or grandfather had the money idle in the bank, but the proposition looked too risky. He declined. The wildcatter found the money somewhere else and struck oil before he had gone another hundred feet.

If it was in the nineteenth century that the ancestor missed the fortune, he missed it by failing to find a lost mine or buried treasure. This was the experience of Adam Lawrence. In 1833 when he was living on a ranch west of the Brazos, an old Spaniard walked up to his cabin one day and said he was sick and needed help. Lawrence cared for him until he was well. Then the Spaniard told him that he had been a member of Lafitte's pirate crew, and that when his master was captured, he and two others were guarding the treasure on Galveston Island some distance from the scene of surrender. They placed the treasure in two small cannon, the gold in one and the silver in the other, and

[24] Ibid.

buried them in the sand 703 varas from a hackberry tree. They took an oath that none of them would try to recover the treasure unless all three were present. They made their escapes, going in different directions.

The Spaniard had recently learned that the other two were dead. Released from his oath, he was on his way to dig up the cannon. If Lawrence would go with him and help him, he would give him half the treasure, and if he would take care of him the rest of his life, he would make him his heir.

On their way to Galveston Island, they camped on November 3. That was the night the stars fell on Texas. In the bright moonlight Lawrence observed the old Spaniard asleep with his shirt open. There was a great scar on his chest. His relaxed face looked inhuman. An owl hooted in a nearby bottom; a timber wolf howled. Lawrence began to wonder. Maybe the old man was the devil leading him to destruction.

All at once the heavens seemed to be on fire; shooting stars were falling all around. Lawrence sprang on his horse and fled for home. He reached it late the next day, exhausted.

About a month later a man came hunting Lawrence. He said that the old Spaniard had died at his cabin a few days after the stars fell, and had given him a package to be delivered to "Señor" Lawrence. The package contained a map of Galveston Island, showing a hackberry tree and a line leading from it marked 703 varas. This Lawrence gave to his wife Sallie, telling her to put it away carefully. He then wrote his brother-in-law, Lindsay Rucker, a surveyor, to join him. But when Rucker arrived Sallie had forgotten where she put the map. They proceeded without it, but found nothing. Many years later a cannon filled with silver was washed up during a storm. The gold must still be there.[25]

If your name is Duarte or Guerra, your family saga will bear

---

[25] Wade, "Tales of Early Texas."

a resemblance to those of the Smiths and the Lawrences. There will perhaps be more emphasis on the supernatural.

It might well include a tale about how the jumping about of the stove led an ancestor to suspect the presence of a ghost; how he consulted his *compadre* as one more learned in such things than he; how the *compadre* concluded that without doubt a ghost was trying to reveal the hiding place of a treasure and that whoever found it must pay the debts of the deceased so that his spirit might have rest; how when the two men were digging under the stove, a voice said, "Whoever takes my fortune takes my debts also"; how they uncovered a chest full of gold; how the *compadre* took it all, promising to pay the ghost's debts and give the other man half the remainder; how when a week had passed and no debts had been paid, the *compadre* was found dead, his mouth full of mud; and how when the chest was opened it contained nothing but mud.[26]

Or your family saga might include a story, as that of the Guerra family does, about the Texas Rangers, "*los rinches*" of the Mexican Border ballads. The Guerras stood for law and order during a long period of international banditry—a banditry in which citizens of both republics were involved, and one which reached a climax during the Civil War and Reconstruction. When Texas was readmitted to the Union, the Ranger force was reorganized and sent to the Border with emphatic orders to suppress crime. Using methods other than passive resistance, they were largely though not wholly successful.

It was during this time that Uncle Pedro Fulano was living on a ranch he had established some miles from Buena Vista, the Guerra home. One day Uncle Pedro missed some horses. He followed their tracks and about nightfall came to a camp where three men had them in their possession. When he demanded his

[26] Guadalupe Duarte, "Around the Fire with My Abuelitos," unpublished manuscript.

property, they opened fire. Unhit, he fired back. He killed one man and the other two fled. He took his horses home and the next day rode to the county seat, reported what he had done, and demanded a trial. He was acquitted.

About a month later two Rangers stopped at the Guerra ranch and asked how they might find Pedro Fulano. They said they wanted to congratulate him upon the bravery he had displayed in the protection of his property. Their host, somewhat suspicious af first, became convinced of their good faith, but he knew that Pedro would probably be alarmed. He told one of his sons to saddle a horse and ride immediately to Uncle Pedro's and prepare him for the visit. In the meantime he insisted that the Rangers stay for supper.

When they reached Uncle Pedro's ranch, he was not there. Two weeks later his wife got a letter saying that he was safe in Mexico. He had found a suitable location, and she was to sell the ranch and join him.

Uncle Pedro's story is told on the Border. It shows how the barbaric "*rinches*" terrified even honest men.[27]

I have attempted by examples to indicate the kind of folklore found in the family saga. Since most of these stories exist in multiple versions and are attached to more than one person, they cannot all be true. A study of the migration of specific stories might be undertaken when more versions are available.

In the meantime the fact of their migration from place to place and from person to person is not difficult to account for.

Listeners, especially children, often confuse narrator and actor. When I was a child, for example, my mother told me the story of the trapped corn thief. This tale concerns a man who, seeing that corn was being taken through a crack in his crib at night, set a steel trap and chained it inside the crib. The next

[27] Fermina Guerra, *Mexican and Spanish Folklore and Incidents in Southwest Texas*, M.A. thesis, University of Texas, 1941, pp. 36–38.

morning he saw a neighbor standing with his hand in the crack. "Good morning, Mr. Blank," he said; "come in and have breakfast."

When I told a neighbor boy how my grandfather had caught a thief in a steel trap, he said it wasn't my grandfather at all. The tale was old hat to him. I questioned my mother and she explained that she had said her father *told* the story. She had *not* said that he was the one who set the trap. Later I was to find the story widely diffused.

Again, characters who are vivid for whatever reason attract stories. One has only to recall such historical personages as Andrew Jackson, Sam Houston, and Abe Lincoln of Illinois—or Peter Cartwright, also of Illinois, who once complained that "almost all those various incidents that had gained currency throughout the country, concerning Methodist preachers, had been located on me."[28]

Finally the very art of narration encourages attribution to persons the narrator knows or knows about. One cannot say, "*A* told me that *B* told him that *C* told him that *D* told him that *E* went on a turkey hunt." If the age and known experience of the narrator are such that he can plausibly say, "I went on a turkey hunt," that is what he is likely to say. Or if he is too young, "My father [or Uncle John, or Grandfather] went on a turkey hunt."

I have chosen my examples from Texas because that is where my work has chiefly been done. But I should like to suggest to folklorists all over America that in the family saga we have an important source of living folklore—a folklore that can be collected with relative ease. Each generation produces a few collectors and raconteurs of the family lore. These can be found and encouraged to talk, sometimes into microphones. Teachers in colleges and universities can put their students to work. Young

---

[28] Peter Cartwright, *Autobiography* (New York, 1856), p. 109.

Americans, like their elders, are searching for a past. They will bring you much chaff but more than enough wheat to compensate for it. Some students get a keen emotional satisfaction in questioning elderly friends and relatives and writing their family lore. If they feel secure in their status they will be honest. They will even tell you the Illinois equivalent of why great-great-great-grandfather came to Texas.

11. The Oil Promoter as Trickster (1961)

Among the archetypical characters in folklore none is more universally known than the trickster—the one who prevails, or sometimes fails to prevail, by his wits. Other archetypes may win by their prowess, by their use of magic, or by the aid of helpers, often animals who spy for them, often supernatural agencies like genii and fairy godmothers. But the trickster's only weapon is his wits, his cleverness, and his only technique is deceit.

He exists in the lore of all cultures, literate and preliterate. He may be the coyote of the North American Indians, the spider of North Africa, the Brer Rabbit of American Negro slaves. He may be a human being like Pedro Urdemales, known to the Spanish-speaking world; like Hans, the unpromising third son of

NOTE: Originally published in *Singers and Story Tellers*, pp. 76–91. Publications of the Texas Folklore Society, no. 30 (Dallas: SMU Press, 1961).

the German peasants; he may be John the southern slave, who gains privileges and escapes punishment by outwitting his master. He may be the Yankee peddler with his wooden nutmegs and his eight-day clock, which runs eight days and then stops forever.

Under one name or another, he is known everywhere, and everywhere commands a mixture of admiration and condemnation. His universal appeal is not easy to account for. It may be assumed that he is in some sense a projection of a quality inherent in the human condition: perhaps of our consciousness of our insufficiencies in our universe;[1] of our intuitive knowledge, if not conscious awareness, of original sin, expressed in the adage that "there is a little larceny in us all"; or of revolt against necessary social restraint.

Sometimes the trickster will have our complete sympathy, sometimes our bitter contempt, and sometimes we rejoice to see the trickster tricked. Our attitude will depend partly upon the motivation of the trickster and partly upon our sympathy or lack of it for his victim. Lazarillo de Tormes resorted to trickery to live, Jack Wilton in order to live merrily, Brer Rabbit sometimes to live and sometimes to live merrily. But the most typical motivation of the trickster is greed .

While certain archetypes seem to survive all cultural changes, they are not themselves unchanged. The knight errant trades his armor and spear for a six-shooter. Cinderella learns a new technique. Her godmother has a big bank account, and may be an industrialist, an oilman, or a movie producer. When it's all three, Cinderella has it made. The trickster no longer sells money-bearing trees to simple country folk, not even gold bricks to country merchants. But the rise of industry, of finance capitalism, and more recently of mass communications has opened doors of opportunity that would have bewildered Pedro Urde-

---

[1] See "Trickster," *Standard Dictionary of Folklore, Mythology and Legend* (New York, 1950).

males or Sam Slick. By no means is the trickster disappearing from our culture and our lore. At mid-century, in his most sophisticated persona, he manipulates symbols of popular value from his Madison Avenue office. But for the first thirty-five years of this century he was most often and most conspicuously an oil promoter.

In a denotative sense, anybody who promotes an oil venture is an oil promoter, but among the oil folk he is one who promotes a venture from which he hopes to gain whether oil is found or not. Whether he sells interests in a well or stock in a company, he expects to be compensated for his trouble, oil or no oil. This is not to say that he always, or indeed in most instances, is a trickster. There were and are legitimate and ethical means of promotion. For a simplified example often used in the past, let us say a promoter secures a lease on a town lot in Breckenridge in 1918. He estimates that he can sink a well to the producing sand for $50,000. He sells seventy-five one-percent interests in the well for $1,000 each. He has $25,000 above the expected cost of the well, and if he finds oil, one-fourth of the seven-eighths remaining after the landowner's royalty has been deducted is his. He hasn't deceived anybody.

He becomes a trickster if he does what many promoters are reported to have done—that is, if he sells interests totaling more that 100 percent. I have been told that two men operating under this plan had the misfortune to strike oil and that they plugged up their wells and left in a hurry.

There is no conclusive reason for assuming that these latter men are more typical of promoters than the first. Nevertheless, they and their kind have cast suspicion upon the whole fraternity. It is significant that Dad Joiner's friends have resented his being called a promoter. They want it understood that he was a bona fide wildcatter seriously looking for oil.

This suspicion dates from the first oil boom, when the gold excitement had somewhat abated and sharp practicers were turning to oil. A musical publisher, taking advantage of the excitement that Drake's well had started, brought out the *Oil on the Brain Songster* in 1865, in which several songs satirize oil promoters. One lists the following companies or partnerships:

FAMOUS OIL FIRMS
By E. Pluribus Oilum

There's "Ketchum and Cheatum,"
And "Lure 'em and Beatum,"
　And "Swindleum" all in a row;
Then "Coax 'em and Lead 'em,"
And "Leech 'em and Bleed 'em,"
　And "Guzzle 'em, Sing 'em and Co."

There's "Gull 'em and Skinner,"
And "Gammon and Sinner,"
　"R. Askal and Oil and Son,"
With "Spongeum and Fleeceum,"
And "Strip 'em and Grease 'em,"
　And the "Take 'em in Brothers and Run."

There's "Watch 'em and Nab 'em,"
And "Knock 'em and Grab 'em,"
　And "Lather and Shave 'em well," too;
There's "Force 'em and Tie 'em,"
And "Pump 'em and Dry 'em,"
　And "Wheedle and Soap 'em" in view.

There's "Pare 'em and Core 'em,"
And "Grind 'em and Bore 'em,"
　And "Pinchum good, Scrapeum and Friend,"
With "Done 'em and Brown 'em,"
And "Finish and Drown 'em,"
　And thus I might go to the end.[2]

Similar ridicule appeared in newspapers and periodicals. The *Boston Commercial* published a burlesque prospectus of The

[2] *Oil on the Brain Songster* (Cincinnati, 1865), p. 19.

Munchausen Philosopher's Stone and Gull Creek Grand Consolidated Oil Company, with a capital stock of four billion dollars, and working capital of $39.50. Dividends were to be paid
semi-daily, except on Sunday. The directors were S. W. Indle,
R. Ascal, D. Faulter (treasurer), S. Teal, Oily Gammon, and
John Law. The *Typographical Advertiser* in the same year
(1865) announced the organization of The Antipodal Petroleum
Company, with a capital stock of one billion dollars, with a par
value of $10,000 per share, but offered to the public at twenty-
five cents. The company proposed to drill through the earth and
obtain production in both the United States and China from a
single well. The treasurer was Mr. Particular Phitts, and the
president was The Hon. Goentoem Strong.[3]

Thirty-five or more years later Texas was to have its quota of
D. Faulters, R. Ascals, and Particular Phitts. In referring to
some of them I have used such terms as "it was said," "it was
reported." Some of my informants have been reluctant to name
names or to give clues to identification. Thus not all my information can be verified, nor does it need to be. I am concerned
with the public image of the trickster-promoter. I shall not attempt to follow in detail the careers of any of the notorious
tricksters exposed in court. It was their tricks that brought great
crowds into the courtrooms, and that led to legendary embellish-
ments of their exploits. It is the type, the persona, that commands our interest. There is, however, sufficient documentary
evidence in the form of newspaper advertising, exposures in
journals, and reports of court trials to suggest that the popular
image has its objective correlative.

The trickster's greed is taken for granted, and a degree of
cleverness—which, however, did not always see him through.
How did he operate? What were his tricks?

The simplest of all was well-salting, a trick he might have

[3] Both quoted in *The Derrick Handbook of Petroleum* (Oil City, Pennsylvania, 1898), vol. 1, pp. 1047–1049.

learned from the gold and silver mine promoters who preceded him. The first salters of whom I have record were a couple of Vermont Yankees lured to Pennsylvania by the first oil boom. In 1864, when Alfred W. Smiley was working as a clerk, a report reached him that an abandoned well had been deepened and was good for twenty or thirty barrels. Smiley went to the well and saw oil flowing into a storage tank. The Vermonters sold the well to a Bostonian for $40,000 cash. The purchaser found that the pumps had been rigged so that oil from the tank flowed back into the well to be pumped back into the tank in an endless cycle. But before this discovery was made the gentlemen from Vermont who had made the sale were "extremely absent." Apparently they were never brought to trial.[4] Thus the country boys triumphed over the city slicker.

This trick, then, seems to have been a Yankee invention, but Texans have not been averse to making use of it. In 1921 John H. Wynne and his partner acquired six sections of land in Reeves County. They had not particularly wanted the land, but had taken it on a debt when money was not forthcoming. Six months later word came that oil had been found near by, and a lease hound offered them five dollars an acre. This was more than they had considered the land worth in fee simple. But instead of signing up, they decided to investigate. Wynne found the well. When the man on duty would open a valve, oil would flow from the casing head. It would be permitted to flow only a few minutes, for, the operator explained, he had no storage. But the driller gave the secret away. The oil flowed from a tank car on the railroad siding near by, and there was enough gas in the well to bring it to the surface. Leasing activity ceased abruptly and Wynne and his partner did not get their $19,200.[5]

This method of salting is rather crude. The more sophisticated

<hr />

[4] Alfred Wildon Smiley, *A Few Scraps (Oily and Otherwise)* (Oil City, 1907), pp. 72–74.

[5] John Wynne, tape-recorded interview, January 26, 1960.

salter leaves the evidence for others to discover or interpret. This is more convincing and less dangerous. He may sprinkle the derrick with crude oil, and if he means to sell stock, he will photograph it. He may pour oil in the slush pit, or bring oil sand from a producing well and leave it on the derrick floor for a scout to find. When Dad Joiner's driller hit the oil sand, he washed the bit in a bucket of water and left it on the derrick floor. The stories resulting from this are too many to recount here. One man told me of going to the derrick and finding it unattended, of examining the sand and finding all the evidence of salting. He joined the legion of East Texans who failed to grasp the forelock that Dad Joiner's discovery provided.

It was inevitable that some well salter would be hoist with his own petard, for wherever there are stories of tricksters, there are stories of the trickster tricked. My story comes from Burkburnett and the operator will be called A. D. Siever. He poured crude into his well and hauled it out with a bailer in the presence of prospective buyers, a couple of New York Jews. They bought, and Siever was happy in his success. To outwit a New Yorker was a considerable achievement, to outwit a Jew was a greater achievement, but to outwit two New Yorkers and two Jews at one and the same time was a superb achievement. But Siever's complacency was short-lived. The New Yorkers deepened the well and brought in a producer worth many times what they had paid for it. And Siever never knew whether his salting sold the well, or whether the buyers had geological information unknown to him.[6]

How extensively well salting was practiced can hardly be known, but both the legal record and the oral tradition would indicate that it played a relatively minor role in dishonest oil promotion. The trickster relied mainly upon the sale of corporate stocks, and his indispensable assets were imagination and verbal

[6] E. M. Everton, oral interview.

skill. Mr. Ecks furnishes an example of what was needed. Hauled into court on a charge of selling fraudulent oil stock, he somehow got access to the witnesses for the prosecution. He sold every one of them a share or more of stock, and agreed to take in payment their vouchers for mileage and witness fees. The judge declared a mistrial. Years later my informant saw Mr. Ecks, who told him that he had suffered his punishment, had repented of his sins and been converted to religion, and was now successfully using his talent in the service of the Lord. He was a revivalist.[7]

My informant was silent upon the name of Mr. Ecks's company, but I am sure it was well chosen. For the trickster knew that a rose by any other name would not smell so sweet to the people on his sucker list.

If the company was a modest one, with holdings limited to a single locality, the trickster often sought a name that would link his company with a producing well or field. For example, the discovery well at Desdemona was on the Duke farm. Eighteen companies used the word *Duke*: The Grand Duke Producing Company, Heart of Duke, Duke Extension, El Paso Duke, Italian Duke, Post Duke, Duke-Burk-Ranger (three fields represented), Duke Knowles Annex, Royal Duke, Duke Consolidated Royalty Syndicate, Erath Duke, Duke Dome, Alma-Duke, Tex-Duke, Giant Duke, Duke of Dublin, Comanche Duke, Iowa Duke.[8] Some of the Dukes were found to be fraudulent, as was also the Blue Bird Oil Company, one of several making use of symbols of luck. Others were Lucky Boy, Lucky Seven, and Rainbow. Uncle Sam suggests patriotism, but the company so named was a notorious swindle. The great supercorporation through which Dr. Frederick A. Cook and Seymour E. J. Cox swindled thousands bore the innocent and cooperative-sounding title of The Petroleum Producers Association.

Another device was to choose a name suggesting an affiliation

[7] James A. Haakerson, oral interview.
[8] Boyce House, *Were You at Ranger?* (Dallas, 1935), p. 116.

between your company and a well-known successful one. Two such companies offering stock for sale during the Beaumont boom were the Rockefeller Oil Company of Beaumont and the Stephenville Standard Oil Company of Beaumont. The only connection they had with John D. Rockefeller or any of his Standard companies was in the names.[9]

The General Lee Development Interests would seem at first sight an inspiration for a corporation seeking to sell stock in Dixie. But the organizers were not content to rely upon the magic of the name. They found a janitor named Robert A. Lee, conferred a military title upon him, declared him a descendant of Robert E. Lee, paid him $12.50 a day for the use of his name, and described him as a famous geologist. Their literature proclaimed that just as "Robert E. Lee gave his life to the South, so is now General Robert A. Lee giving his life to the oil industry and the cause of humanity." But a federal court found that he was no kin to Marse Robert, and that he was not a geologist. Nor was the jury convinced that he was giving his life to the cause of humanity. He and sponsors paid fines and went to a federal prison.[10]

During the heyday of the oil trickster, from 1918 to 1924, radio and television were not available, but he had other means of getting his message to the public. One was to get his propaganda published in reputable papers as news. A notorious example is a story that appeared in the *New York Sun* in 1903 (May 10). Whether payola was involved, my sources do not reveal.

Under the 200 square miles of rolling prairie land controlled by Mr. King and his associates, there is a vast sea of petroleum. While its length and breadth have been pretty well established, no plummet has ever yet sounded its depths.

It lies in its subterranean bed, where it will sleep until the

[9] Boyce House, *Oil Boom* (Caldwell, Idaho, 1941), p. 32.
[10] *New York Times*, May 9, 1923.

suction pumps of the big King-Crowther Corporation begin to thud and clank in the oil-filled caves. As yet, the surface has been barely scratched, as it were, and seven wells have been found. By a fair process of reason, it may be assumed that in the entire 200 square miles of territory, when fully developed, there should be at least 8000 oil wells.

The general idea is to pay the investor not less than 20% a year so that in five years he will receive his original investment, leaving a profit of from three to five times the original amount.

These estimates are based on Mr. King's knowledge and experience. As a matter of fact, investments may pay anywhere from three to five times in excess of the figures quoted.[11]

A few days after this story appeared, the attorney general of Texas filed a petition alleging that the King-Crowther Corporation had obtained its charter through false information. The court estimated that shareholders had been fleeced out of two million dollars.

As newspapers grew more wary of publishing free advertising, the trickster, knowing the advantage of the seemingly impartial news story, began acquiring control of oil journals by founding, by purchase, or by lending them money. The *World's Work*, in an article exposing fraud in the oil industry (1923),[12] listed eleven periodicals as owned or controlled by oil promoters: *Pat Morris Oil News (Fearless and Truthful Oil News)*, *Independent Oil and Financial Reporter (Fair, Faithful and Fearless)*, *International Investors Bulletin*, *Independent Oil News*, *Texas Oil World*, *Texas Oil Ledger*, *National Oil Journal*, *Arkansas Oil and Mineral News*, the *Banker, Merchant, and Manufacturer*, *Mining and the Industrial Age*, and *Commercial and Financial World*. It was charged that one of these was for a time hos-

[11] *Oil Investors' Journal* 2 (June 1, 1903): 5.
[12] J. K. Barnes, "Doctor Cook's Discovery of Oil," *World's Work* 45 (April 1923): 611–617.

tile to Dr. Cook, but was brought to see the light by a substantial loan.

But not all tricksters could afford an independent oil journal. They relied chiefly on newspaper advertising and direct mailing. In spite of the better business bureaus and the Vigilance Committee of the Associated Advertising Clubs of the World,[13] which in 1921 declared that 95 percent of oil stock offered through newspapers was unworthy, it was still possible to get wide coverage. Because security laws were more lax than now and because both the post office and attorney general's department were grossly understaffed, fear of legal action was not a wholly effective deterrent, a fact which gave vigor and scope to the imagination.

The *New York Times* (March 9, 1924), commenting particularly on conditions in Texas and more specifically in Fort Worth, known as the capital of fraudulent oil promotion, observed that the oil stock promoter "has contributed some of the glibbest, most convincing writing of our era. Some of this writing is so broad and highly colored that the secret story should be plain to see. But the public is greedy for this sort of fiction, and the oil stock frauds flourish in the fertile soil of the public imagination."

A sampling of this writing tends to support the judgment of the *Times* editorialist. There were a number of approaches, each with its appropriate style and tone. One might be called the unqualified promise, delivered in bold, simple, and direct English:

> Oil will always be in demand, it will always yield its fixed, profitable price, and it will make dividends to the holders of shares in the Bonnabel Refining Company as sure and steady as the progression of time. . . . The company can guarantee at least 20% per annum.[14]

[13] "Investing in Oil," *Review of Reviews* 63 (April 1921): 443.
[14] *Oil Investors' Journal* 3 (October 15, 1904): 7.

I absolutely guarantee $200 returned for every $100 loaned
me for oil development, with a full 100% profit remaining as a
permanent investment.[15]

"Conservative estimate of profits . . . 350%." On the inside
cover of the prospectus was the following unacknowledged quotation:

> Our doubts are traitors,
> They make us lose the good
> We might win by fearing to attempt.[16]

One syndicate "aimed at" 10,000 percent profit in from four
to six months.[17]

Such statements as these are what the *Times* writer had in
mind as so broad and highly colored as to give the secret away.
One could sound more convincing by promising big profits and
then adding qualifications that would leave the profits still big.
One promoter had a tract of a hundred acres upon which he said
there was room for fifty wells.

> Even if these fifty wells should make *only* 100 barrels apiece,
> the oil, being Pennsylvania grade, commands a price of $4 per
> barrel at the well, and will net us a nice profit . . . 50 times 100
> will be 50,000 barrels a day, which at $4 per barrel, will equal
> $200,000 a day. This multiplied by 300 [perhaps the wells were
> not to produce on Sundays and holidays] will make a total in-
> come of $60,000,000 a year from this 100 acres alone.

But he goes on to say that 10 wells would be sufficient to develop
the property, and, even if the production were only 25 barrels
per well, the income would still be $300,000 a year.[18]

Another theme is: others have got rich, why not you? Often

[15] House, *Oil Boom*, p. 26.

[16] *Oil Investors' Journal* 3 (May 3, 1905): 9.

[17] Barnes, "Doctor Cook's Discovery of Oil," *World's Work* 45 (April
1923): 611–617.

[18] *Current Opinion* 70 (April 21, 1921): 545.

there was the warning that you had better hurry, for the stock is going up!

ARKANSAS GIRL MAKES $300,000 ON OIL ACREAGE.
BUYS LAND FOR $500; REALIZES $900,000; BIG PROFIT, EH, WHAT?
THREE MEN POOLED THEIR ALL, $25, AND SOLD FOR $250,000.[19]

Others preferred a tone of frankness. There is risk in the oil business:

If you ask my advice about investing, I don't give any. I have acted on my own judgment, and have invested in the Company with which I am identified. I don't advise anybody either one way or the other. If we strike oil our stock will be worth ten to one, or more. If we don't strike a well there will be no difficulty in selling our holdings at a greatly advanced price, as values are doubling, quadrupling and quintupling there from day to day. I determined, however, that I would give nobody advice in the matter. If I should give the advice and our stockholders made a thousand per cent on the investment, they would think I was a great man; but if I gave the advice, and there was nothing made out of the investment, they would lay the failure in the realization of their fast profits, to my account. I shall accumulate no such liabilities as these. I have unbounded faith in the oil fields there, and I believe they are going to supply the fuel and the illumination for the world; but I don't advise anybody either one way or the other. I can only say this: If any readers . . . are going to buy oil stock, our oil stock is as good as any oil stock in the market and far better than ninety per cent that is being sold.[20]

If you cannot afford to take a chance to lose $10 to $25, do not go into this scheme because oil investments are uncertain. Admittedly it is a "long shot." The backers of the company have

[19] *Literary Digest* 77 (December 8, 1923): 11.
[20] *Baptist Standard*, May 2, 1901.

such a firm belief in it, based on the best geological information obtainable, that they have put their own money into it.[21]

In our exaltation of the hero we have sometimes without the warrant of fact made every discovery somebody's folly. There was Columbus' folly, Fulton's folly, Morse's folly, and in oil, Drake's folly and Higgins' folly, and if we may trust a newspaper advertisment, Carruth's folly. One of his ads ran:

> Hog Creek Carruth: The name that will live throughout the ages as the name of the man who toiled singlehanded for seven long years to prove up his belief and attain his goal—who traced an oil structure 20 miles across the ranges from Strawn to Desdemona—who conceived and organized the famous Hog Creek Oil Co.—who drilled the discovery well of the great Desdemona field at one time called the richest spot on earth—who transformed a desert into a fountain of liquid gold—who built a city of 30,000 souls from a village of 200 people and who paid every person who held shares of stock in his renowned Hog Creek Co. \$10,133 for every \$100 invested.[22]

Thus were the doubting Thomases confounded.

One very successful copy writer found the folksy style effective:

> Now, folks, I'm going to tell you a lot of things in this ad that will be good for your souls. I'm not a promoter and I'm not an ad writer—I'm just plain old Harry Bleam. All I can do is just sit down and tell you this stuff the way I know it to be. Most everybody knows about Harry Bleam. I'm just a common guy. I'm not in politics, but I'm a square shooter from who laid the chunk, and I put my cards down on the table face up. I'm not a promoter. You will know that anyway in just a minute, because I'm going to tell you something no promoter ever told

[21] "Investing in Oil," *Review of Reviews* 63 (April 1921): 443–444.
[22] *New York Times*, March 9, 1924.

you. If the well I'm getting ready to drill on my big little 4-acre tract down there don't come in a gusher, then there ain't no such thing as a bellyache. . . .

Why, if I didn't believe I was going to get oil here—and I don't mean just a dinky little 1,000 barrel well—I mean a 10,000 or 15,000 barrel well—I'd never try to sell anybody an interest in it. . . .[23]

Boyce House tells of a promoter whose literature showed a picture of a cell block at the Leavenworth Prison underneath which was the statement, "The doors of this prison will open to receive ———— ———— if he fails to make good every statement made to the public."[24] This statement is no mean achievement. But Dr. Cook could visualize a worse fate. Here he describes his thoughts while watching an oil-well fire:

I stood on a hill about a half a mile away watching this shaft of light and heat as its wicked tongues of flame leaped and roared while the men rushed around in their feverish haste to extinguish this great torch of the oil fields. I was standing there with the black of the night behind me and the clear white light of this burning well in front of me, wondering if possibly all this roaring fire wasn't in reality sent as a kind of warning to the fake promoters—the meanest rodents that ever breathed God's pure air.

I don't believe that a man who would wilfully defraud the public and take from the investors who are willing to help develop nature's resources the money which they have so carefully saved, without giving them a fair return, deserves much better an end that might be typified by this flaming gas well.

The preachers tell me that the day of fire and brimstone in the church is past but we have plenty of it left in the oil fields and I wonder after all if his Satanic Majesty isn't retaining just

[23] *Fort Worth Star-Telegram*, January 15, 1922.
[24] House, *Oil Boom*, pp. 56–57.

a little supply of the old fashioned hell-fire torment for the reception of a few phony promoters.[25]

Whatever the ultimate fate of Dr. Cook, a cell block at Leavenworth did open to receive him.

What the promoter trickster's take was can only be hinted at. Within eight months after the Spindletop discovery, the capitalization of Texas oil companies had reached $231,000,000, although actual investment in the Beaumont field was estimated at only $11,000,000.[26] Within a year there were five hundred Texas oil companies doing business in Beaumont, not to mention hundreds more chartered in other states.[27] Not wholly untypical were four companies capitalized at one million each. Their assets were a jointly held lease on a block of land forty-five feet square.[28] It is little wonder that Spindletop became known as Swindletop.

Carl Coke Rister says that out of 1,050 new stock companies formed in 1918-19, only seven paid dividends. The Oklahoma Commission of Corporations estimated that only one dollar was returned out of every $550 invested in stock companies. In Kansas it was estimated that in 1916-17 only 12 of 1,500 new companies showed profits. An Oklahoma writer estimated that there had been a $555 capitalization for every barrel of oil produced.[29] In 1924 the *Financial World* estimated that the capital of defunct oil companies had aggregated $500,000,000.[30] Rister esti-

[25] Barnes, "Doctor Cook's Discovery of Oil," *World's Work* 45 (April 1923): 614–615.

[26] House, *Oil Boom*, p. 31.

[27] James A. Clark and Michel T. Halbouty, *Spindletop* (New York, 1952), p. 87.

[28] House, *Oil Boom*, p. 31.

[29] Carl Coke Rister, *Oil! Titan of the Southwest* (Norman, 1949), pp. 185–188.

[30] Wirt Hord, *Lost Dollars, or Pirates of Promotion* (Cincinnati, 1924), p. 13.

mates a total accumulated investment of $102,000,000,000 up to 1947, against a return of $61,000,000,000.[31]

It is not to be assumed that all, or even a majority, of the unsuccessful companies were fraudulent. But there are indications that the aggregate sum that went into the pockets of the tricksters was considerable. The *World's Work* in 1918 said that one promoter (he was jailed) had fleeced 25,000 people out of $2,500,000.[32] In February, 1924, there were in federal courts sixty-three cases pending against persons representing or claiming to represent Texas oil companies, who, the Department of Justice claimed, had taken in $140,000,000. A year earlier the solicitor general of the Post Office Department estimated that during the preceding five years $100,000,000 had been lost to fraudulent promoters in Texas alone: "No doubt some of these companies were started by men who hoped to strike oil and make money from the production, but in practically every case the promoters had laid their plans to profit from stock selling, regardless of the result of field operations. Seldom was it that a promoter invested his own money."[33]

The great crackdown came in 1923. The Securities and Exchange laws of the 1930s made it considerably more difficult for the trickster to operate. I would not be so bold as to say that he has left the oil industry altogether, but his heyday in this industry is over.

A convicted bank robber once made this defense of his trade: When he robbed a bank, nobody lost a dollar but the insurance company, and it obviously gained in the long run; for if the bank robbing ceased, the sale of robbery insurance would cease soon afterward.

I know of no such ingenious defense having been made of the oil trickster. When he was brought to trial, he typically pled

---

[31] Rister, *Oil! Titan of the Southwest*, p. 394.
[32] *World's Work* 27 (November, 1918): 510.
[33] *New York Times*, April 7, 1923.

guilty. When he pled not guilty, he was an honest man who had exposed himself to the hazards of the business in a sincere effort to help his fellow-man. If, in imitation of the bank robber, he had attempted to rationalize his conduct, he might have said that his social role was to alleviate the disastrous economic effects of oversaving. But Keynesian economics was not in fashion in the days of Harding and Coolidge and Hoover.

12. Theodore Roosevelt, Social Darwinism, and the Cowboy (1964)

At the turn of the century there were no market research agencies or public opinion polls to tell a publisher who his customers were. But it has been plausibly surmised that firms like Street and Smith, Beadle and Adams knew the audience they were aiming at and that they reached it—an audience consisting chiefly of people who through the expanding public schools had acquired the ability to read on an elementary level but had made little use of this ability until works appeared on the newsstands addressed particularly to them: "soldiers, sailors, lumberjacks, hired girls, adolescent boys."[1] These latter, if they were of middle-class background, followed the adventures of

NOTE: Originally published in *Texas Quarterly* 7 (winter 1964): 11–20.
[1] Merle Curti, "Dime Novels and the American Tradition," *Yale Review* 22 (summer 1932): 761.

Deadwood Dick, Nick Carter, Buffalo Bill, Buck Taylor, and Chris Comstock without parental blessing.[2]

Before the cowboy could reach adults of the genteel middle class, he had to be presented on a slightly, but only slightly, more sophisticated level. But more important, he had to be assimilated to the current social mythology of this increasingly urbanized class. Highly influential in bringing about this synthesis were two Harvard graduates who reached the cattle West by train in the 1880s: Theodore Roosevelt interpreted the cowboy in terms of the dominant social philosophy of the period, and Owen Wister embodied Roosevelt's interpretation in fiction sponsored by respectable publishers and read by respectable readers.[3]

Obviously pleased with the reception accorded him on his tour of the western states in 1903, Roosevelt wrote John Hay that at every small city and country town he was "greeted by the usual shy, self-conscious local committeemen, and spoke to the usual audience of thoroughly good Americans." He reported that the greater part of his audience consisted of "rough-coated hard-headed, gaunt, and sinewy farmers and hired hands from all the neighborhood, who had driven in with their wives and children; from ten or twenty or even thirty miles round about."

"For all the superficial differences between us [Roosevelt continued] down at bottom these men and I think a great deal alike, or at least have the same ideals, and I am sure of reaching them in speeches many of my Harvard friends would think not only homely, but commonplace."[4] Roosevelt was to learn in 1912 that this rapport would not continue indefinitely, but for a dozen or

[2] Edmund Pearson in *Dime Novels* (Boston, 1929), pp. 222–255, lists a number of more or less prominent Americans who read dime novels during adolescence.

[3] See my "The American Myth Rides the Range: Owen Wister's Man on Horseback," *Southwest Review* 36 (summer 1951): 157–163.

[4] *Cowboys and Kings: Three Great Letters of Theodore Roosevelt*, with an introduction by Elting E. Morrison (Cambridge, Mass., 1954), p. 2.

so years beginning in 1898, he, better than any other public figure, expressed and symbolized the ideas and ideals of the majority of Americans.

One conspicuous way in which he reflected the folk attitudes
of the time was in his exaltation of the doer over the thinker. He
told college students that "the first great lesson [they] should
learn is the lesson of work rather than criticism." "It is the doer
of deeds who actually counts in the battle for life, and not the
man who looks on and says how the fight ought to be fought."[5]
He thought Admiral Mahan a great man, but considered Henry
George "an utterly cheap reformer."[6] He did not reckon John
Hay among the great secretaries of state. "He had a very ease-
loving nature," and his usefulness as a statesman was impaired
by his association with Henry James and Henry Adams.[7] The
virtues of James and Adams were not the "manly" virtues that
Roosevelt seldom missed an opportunity to extol in terms much
like those of the athletic coach and the scoutmaster. "If we wish
to do good work for our country we must be unselfish, dis-
interested, sincerely desirous of the well being of the common-
wealth, and capable of adherence to a lofty ideal; but in addition
we must be vigorous in mind and body, able to suffer punishment without flinching, and, at need, repay it in kind with interest."[8]

The tone of this advice does not necessarily imply a scrupulous observance of judicial process, which, in theory if not always in practice, calls for unhurried deliberation, a careful
weighing of the evidence, and a reasoned application of law or
principle. If Roosevelt did not advocate extralegal procedures, he

[5] "Colleges and Public Life," *American Ideals and Other Essays* (New York, 1897), p. 51.

[6] Roosevelt to Brander Matthews, November 2, 1895; quoted by Henry F. Pringle, *Theodore Roosevelt: A Biography* (New York, 1931), p. 112.

[7] Roosevelt to Henry Cabot Lodge, January 28, 1909; quoted by Pringle, *Theodore Roosevelt*, p. 243.

[8] "Morality and Efficiency," *American Ideals and Other Essays*, p. 42.

was tolerant of them when they were invoked in behalf of causes he approved. A few days after the Haymarket riot in Chicago he wrote from his ranch in Dakota Territory:

> My men here are hardworking laboring men who work long-er hours for no greater pay than many strikers; but they are Americans through and through; I believe nothing would give them greater pleasure than a chance with their rifles at one of the mobs. When we get papers, especially in relation to the dynamite business, they become more furious and angry than I do. I wish them with me, and a fair show at ten times our number of rioters, my men shoot well and fear very little.[9]

And he liked "to see a mob [presumably of laboring men and populists] handled by regulars, or by good State guards, not over scrupulous about bloodshed."[10]

He seemed to approve of the putting down of "dangerous characters, often by the most summary exercise of lynch law."

> Notorious bullies and murderers have been taken out and hung, while the bands of horse and cattle thieves have been regularly hunted down and destroyed in pitched fights by parties of armed cowboys; and as a consequence most of the ter-ritory is now perfectly law abiding. . . . A little over two years ago one committee of vigilantes in eastern Montana shot or hung nearly sixty—not, however, with the best of judgment in all cases.[11]

If Roosevelt mirrored the folkways of his time in exalting ac-tion over deliberation, he mirrored them also in his adherence to a lingering primitivism. With the closing of the frontier the American people, feeling, even before Turner told them, that they had a history of their own, exalted pioneer virtues and

---

[9] *The Letters of Theodore Roosevelt*, selected and edited by Elting E. Mor-rison (Cambridge, Mass., 1951), pp. 100–101. Hereafter cited as *Letters*.

[10] *Letters*, vol. 1, p. 42.

[11] *Ranch Life and the Hunting Trail* (New York, 1902), p. 14.

looked with nostalgic longing—a longing that Buffalo Bill was making capital of—upon the good old days when life was both simple and heroic. For Roosevelt his ranching experience had taken place in "the golden days when men of the vanishing frontier still lived in the Viking age."[12]

> It is the life of men who live in the open, who tend their herds on horseback, who go armed and ready to guard their lives by their own prowess, who call no man master. Ranching is an occupation like those of vigorous, primitive pastoral peoples, having little in common with the humdrum, workaday business world of the nineteenth century.[13]

Roosevelt admitted that it "was right and necessary that this life should pass, for the safety of our country lies in its being made the country of the small home-maker," and that "the days of 'free grass' necessarily represented a temporary stage in our history,"[14] but he saw those days as a heroic age to be idealized and cherished in memory.

Roosevelt's social philosophy reflected the popular naïve Darwinism of the turn of the century. The debate over the theological implications of natural selection largely subsided with the publication of White's *The Warfare between Science and Theology in Christendom* in 1896. The theological issue had not been of great interest to the masses and would not be a subject of wide popular discussion until after World War I. The experience of the American people had prepared them to accept the postulates of struggle and survival as the way of life. If they read Roosevelt's *The Winning of the West*, they were not shocked to find social evolution advanced as the key to their history. In various enterprises, from establishing a home in the West to founding great businesses, they had seen some succeed

---

[12] *Cowboys and Kings*, p. 1.

[13] *Ranch Life and the Hunting Trail, Works* (National Edition), vol. 1, p. 274.

[14] *Autobiography, Works* (National Edition), vol. 20, p. 98.

and others fail. But the role of the supernatural in popular religion had been so delimited that, unlike an earlier generation, they did not associate success and failure with God's pleasure and displeasure. The winner was somehow better equipped to win.

Roosevelt applied the Spencerian doctrine of struggle and survival of the fittest to the individual, the nation, and the race; and the same qualities were required of each. On all levels survival depended ultimately on force: force applied or force in being, ready for application. The citizen must remain physically vigorous, courageous, alert; the nation must maintain large armaments backed by a citizenry ready to fight for the national interest and the national honor; the race should not only bear sufficient children to offset the high birth rate of the inferior races but should extend their domain over these races. Proof of their inferiority was their inability to form nations. Among superior peoples race and nation tended to become synonymous. A race possessed mental characteristics, a collective soul, which was a synthesis of the sentiments and ideals of the present representatives of the race and those of their ancestors. This collective soul was the product of a long process of inbreeding, which is possible only among people of similar ethnic stocks. In America North and Western European stocks had so blended, and Roosevelt regretted that a similar amalgam of the white races had not taken place in South Africa.[15]

---

[15] *Letters*, vol. 1, p. 253. Roosevelt's racial views do not require extensive documentation here. The evidence that he adhered to the theories of Henry Cabot Lodge, Andrew Carnegie, Sir Walter Besant, and Gustave Le Bon is conclusive. In *The Winning of the West* he justified the displacement of the Indians on social-evolutionary grounds, and he once said, "I don't go so far as to think that the only good Indians are dead Indians, but I believe nine out of ten are, and I should not inquire too closely into the case of the tenth" (Hagedorn, *Roosevelt in the Bad Lands*, p. 355). He wrote Lodge: "What Le Bon says about race is very fine and true" (*Letters*, vol. 1, p. 335). He felt that the Negro had been "kept down as much by lack of intellectual develop-

Roosevelt, no more than Spencer, saw in evolution a sanction of a tooth and claw struggle. Again, he reflected the values of his countrymen in maintaining the validity of moral law without being curious about its ultimate source; it was one of the given facts of life. In international affairs, each nation pursued its own interests. German expansion was right for Germany, but other nations were right in opposing it.[16] In business a monopoly that was established and maintained without violating the moral law was a good monopoly, but he recognized the difficulty in applying the moral law to the impersonal corporation. His proposed solution was the establishment of a commission to define and enforce ethical practices.[17]

A moral law that assigns primary value to survival is ambiguous. (Does survival mean remaining alive? Does it include maintaining property rights and putting your competitor out of business?) It would in any event place great stress on Roosevelt's "manly virtues" and condone violence as a means of survival. Hagedorn quotes a friend of Roosevelt's "who had himself committed almost every crime in the register," as saying "Roosevelt had a weakness for murderers."[18] Roosevelt denied

---

ment as anything else; but the prime factor in the preservation of a race is its power to attain a high degree of social efficiency" (*American Ideals*, p. 327). He though "the salvation of the Negro lay in the development of the Booker Washington theory—that of fitting him to do ever better in industrial work" (*Letters*, vol. 2, p. 1169). He attributed the alleged cowardice of Negro troops in Cuba "to the superstition and fear of the darky, natural in those but one generation from slavery and but a few generations removed from the wildest savagery" (*Letters*, vol. 2, p. 1305). One basis of his imperialism was his conviction that "it is good for the world that the English-speaking race in all its branches should hold as much of the world's surface as possible (*Letters*, vol. 1, p. 1176–1177).

[16] Roosevelt to Cecil Arthur Spring Rice, August 13, 1897. *Letters*, vol. 1, p. 644.

[17] "The Trust, the People, and the Square Deal," *Outlook* 99, no. 12 (November 18, 1911): 649–656.

[18] Herman Hagedorn, *Roosevelt in the Bad Lands* (New York, 1921), p. 47. 47.

that he favored men who commit crimes, but he said that the man who has paid his penalty, who reforms and makes good should be respected.[19]

But in speaking and writing about some of his western friends, particularly the Rough Riders, he seemed to take more pride in their sinful past than in their present state of grace. Among the Rough Riders were some "who mayhap stood out with a more evil prominence as himself a dangerous man—one given to taking life on small provocation, or one who was ready to earn his living outside the law if occasion demanded it."[20] In a letter to John Hay in 1903, he writes with tolerant amusement about some of his Rough Rider friends who have run afoul of the law, and mentions going to the canyon of the Colorado with "an assorted collection of Rough Riders, most of them with a homicidal past."[21]

These men, whatever their faults, were not pussyfooters and mollycoddles, and therefore not a threat to America. The major threat, as Roosevelt saw it, was an overrefinement, a softening of character, a creeping decadence, manifesting itself among the business classes by an overconcern for money and among intellectuals by cosmopolitanism and expatriation. When Americans confronted the wilderness and its aboriginal inhabitants, the struggle for survival developed a hardy, robust, and independent citizenry. With the frontier rapidly vanishing in 1885 and gone by 1890, with more and more people following sedentary occupations and working routinely in mines and factories, how would it be possible to foster the manly virtues that had made America great? Roosevelt did not succumb to the despair of Brooks Adams or Gustave Le Bon. By precept and example he urged the American people to lead a strenuous life. "It is an admirable thing [he said] to possess refinement and cultivation,

---

[19] *Autobiography*, p. 131.
[20] *The Rough Riders, Works* (Memorial Edition), vol. 13, p. 22.
[21] *Cowboys and Kings*, p. 2.

but the price is too dear if they must be paid for at the cost of the rugged fighting qualities which make a man able to do a man's work."[22]

He did not "undervalue for a moment our material prosperity" but warned that a wealthy nation "slothful, timid, or unwieldy, is an easy prey for any people which still retains the most valuable of all qualities, the soldierly virtues,"[23] and he thought that "we in the United States . . . suffer from all the evils attendant upon our luxurious civilization."[24] What Roosevelt regarded as the duty of men of leisure class is implicit in his statement that he would "regard it an unspeakable disgrace if [any of his sons] failed to work hard at any honest occupation for a livelihood, while at the same time keeping himself in such trim that he would be able to perform a freeman's duty and fight as efficiently as anyone if need arose."[25]

But for the nation at large the soldierly virtues should be cultivated by militarism: preparation for war, and war, for which he sought no moral equivalent. For in Roosevelt's militaristic utterances, much stress is laid on war as fostering the highest moral values. He professed to "abhor violence and bloodshed,"[26] but there were other things he abhorred more. During the Philippine war he was "not in the least sensitive about killing any number of men if there is adequate reason,"[27] and he had previously told his audience at the Naval War College: "No triumph of peace is quite so great as the supreme triumphs of war. The courage of the soldier, the courage of the statesman who has to meet the storms which can be quelled only by soldierly virtues—this stands higher than any quality called out

[22] *American Ideals*, p. 241.

[23] Address to the Naval War College, June 2, 1897; quoted by Pringle, *Theodore Roosevelt*, p. 172.

[24] Pringle, *Theodore Roosevelt*, p. 408.

[25] *Cowboys and Kings*, p. 85.

[26] *Autobiography*, p. 212.

[27] Pringle, *Theodore Roosevelt*, p. 579.

merely in time of peace."[28] And in advocating war with Spain in 1897, he had mentioned "the benefit done to our own people by giving them something to think about which isn't material gain."[29]

Given Roosevelt's delight in having lived in the "Viking Age," his adolescent joy in vigorous physical activity, his impatience with speculative thought, his social Darwinism, which made individual, national, and racial survival ultimately dependent upon force, and his consequent militarism, it is not surprising that he found in the cowboys he knew in the Dakotas those soldierly qualities he identified with good Americanism and that he should defend them against their detractors.

> They are [he wrote in *Ranch Life and Hunting Trail*] small- and less muscular than the wielders of ax and pick; but they are as hardy and self-reliant as any men who ever breathed— with bronzed, set faces, and keen eyes that look all the world straight in the face without flinching as they flash out from under the broad-brimmed hats. Peril and hardship, and years of long toil broken by weeks of brutal dissipation, draw haggard lines across their eager faces, but never dim their reckless eyes nor break their bearing of defiant self-confidence. They do not walk well, partly because their *chaparajos* or leather overalls hamper them when on the ground; but their appearance is striking for all that, and picturesque too, with their jingling spurs, the big revolvers stuck in their belts, and bright silk handkerchiefs knotted loosely round their necks over the open collars of the flannel shirts. When drunk on the villainous whisky of the frontier towns, they cut mad antics, riding their horses into the saloons, firing their pistols right and left, from boisterous lightheartedness rather than from any viciousness, and indulging too often in deadly shooting affrays, brought on

[28] Address to the Naval War College, in Pringle, *Theodore Roosevelt*, p. 172.
[29] Roosevelt to Secretary Long, November 18, 1897; quoted by Pringle, *Theodore Roosevelt*, p. 176.

either by the accidental contact of the moment or on account of some long-standing grudge, or perhaps because of bad blood between two ranches or localities; but except while on such sprees they are quiet, rather self-contained men, perfectly frank and simple, and on their own ground treat a stranger with the most whole-souled hospitality, doing all in their power for him and scorning to take any reward in return. Although prompt to resent an injury, they are not at all apt to be rude to outsiders, treating them with what can almost be called a grave courtesy. They are much better fellows and pleasanter companions than small farmers or agricultural laborers; nor are the mechanics and workmen of a great city to be mentioned in the same breath.[30]

But Roosevelt's high regard for cowboys is expressed most emphatically, not in this and similar public defenses, but in his behavior among them. He clearly wished to be accepted as one of them. And in spite of his strange ways—he did not smoke or drink; his greatest oath was "by Godfrey"; he wore large-lensed glasses; and he spoke a dialect never heard before in the Bad Lands—he won that acceptance. There was great laughter when he ordered a cowboy to "hasten forward quickly there." This Harvard way of saying "Head that cow" became a byword throughout the Bad Lands, but the spirit in which he took the laughter did much to break down the polite reserve the men had maintained toward him.[31] Later he was to prove his mettle by knocking out with his fist a bully who drew his guns and insisted that "Old Four Eyes set up drinks to the crowd,"[32] and by following and arresting, with the help of two of his men, three horse thieves.[33]

Roosevelt became a competent cowhand, though he never

---

[30] *Ranch Life and the Hunting Trail* (New York, 1902), pp. 9–10.

[31] Hagedorn, *Roosevelt in the Bad Lands* (New York, 1921), p. 101.

[32] *Autobiography*, pp. 124–127; Hagedorn, *Roosevelt in the Bad Lands*, pp. 151–154.

[33] *Letters*, vol. 1, p. 98.

made claims of expertness. "I never became a good roper," he said, "nor more than an average rider, according to ranch standards."[34] He preferred to break his own horses, "doing it gently and gradually,"[35] for he never learned to "ride an unbroken horse with comfort."[36] Nevertheless when mounts were being formed, he drew lots with his men for first choice, and chose in his turn.[37] If a bad horse fell to his lot, he accepted him. More than once he was thrown. Once he landed on a stone and fractured a rib, and once his shoulder was injured by a horse's falling over backwards with him.[38]

He wished to live up to the traditions of the range, where a man "does not shirk things merely because they are disagreeable or irksome."[39] His letters, particularly those to his sister Anna and to his close friend Henry Cabot Lodge, reveal the pride he took in making a hand along with his men and in sharing their hardships. On May 15, 1885, he writes that he has just returned from taking a thousand head of cattle up the trail. He has had "hard work and a good deal of fun." "The weather was very bad and I had my hands full, day and night, and not being able to take off my clothes but once during the week out."[40] Later in the season (June 23) he wrote that the roundup was swinging over from the east to the west divide. "Yesterday I was in the saddle at 2 A.M., and except for two very hasty meals, after each of which I took a fresh horse, did not stop working till 8:15 P.M., and was up at half past three in the morning. The eight hour law does not apply to the cowboy."[41]

[34] *Autobiography*, p. 107.
[35] Ibid.
[36] *Letters*, vol. 1, p. 90.
[37] Lincoln A. Lang, *Ranching with Roosevelt* (Philadelphia and London, 1926), p. 183.
[38] *Autobiography*, p. 108; Lang, *Ranching with Roosevelt*, p. 183–184.
[39] *Autobiography*, p. 108.
[40] *Letters*, vol. 1, p. 90.
[41] Ibid., p. 91.

The next season he wrote on June 7 that he had been on the roundup for a fortnight. When it started there "were sixty men. . . . Every one a bold rider, and every one on a good horse." "It has been great fun," he continued, "but hard work—fourteen to sixteen hours every day. Breakfast comes at three; and I am pretty sleepy all the time."[42] By June 28 the roundup was over. It had been five weeks since he had had breakfast later than four o'clock in the morning. "You would hardly know my sun-burned and wind roughened face. But I really enjoyed it and am as tough as a hickory knot."[43]

Besides making a hand in the performance of routines of cow work, Roosevelt gladly exposed himself to the extra hazards that came his way. Once when the Little Missouri was in flood he started across on a submerged dam. In the middle of the stream his horse lost his footing and horse and rider were "swallowed up by the brown waters. . . . Roosevelt flung himself from the horse . . . and with one hand on the horn of the saddle, fended off the larger blocks of ice." Safely out with his glasses still on, he admitted that what he had done "might be considered reck-less. But it was fun."[44] Another time he rode in pitch black dark-ness, relieved now and then by flashes of lightning, during a stampede. Following the cattle by sound, he rode down a steep embankment, and his horse somehow managed to stay on its feet. Later it turned a somersault and threw him. Roosevelt re-mounted and struggled through quicksand to the bank. The horse of another rider was killed by running into a tree.[45]

But nothing speaks more emphatically of Roosevelt's delight in cowboy life and his approval of the cowboy than his elaborate and expensive costumes. He wrote his sister, "I wear a sombrero, silk neckerchief, fringed buckskin shirt, sealskin chaparajos, or

[42] Ibid., p. 102.
[43] Ibid., p. 104.
[44] Hagedorn, *Roosevelt in the Bad Lands*, pp. 251–252.
[45] Ibid., pp. 295–297.

riding trousers, alligator hide boots, and with my pearl-hilted re-
volver and my beautifully finished Winchester rifle, I shall be
able to face anything."[46] He also mentioned his horse, "a superb
pony, or rather horse; he looks well with his beautifully carved
saddle, plaited bridle, and silver inlay bit." In a letter to Lodge
he lists silver spurs among other items of equipment.[47]

Interviewed by a reporter for the *New York Tribune* as he
was about to return to Dakota in July 1884 he said,

> On my last trip I was just three weeks at the ranch and just
> twenty-one days, of sixteen hours each in the saddle, taking
> part in the "round-up," or hunting. It would electrify some
> of my friends who have accused me of representing the kid-
> gloved element in politics if they could see me galloping over
> the plains, day in and day out, clad in buckskin shirt and
> leather chaparajos, with a big sombrero on my head. For good
> healthy exercise I would strongly recommend some of our
> gilded youth go West and try a short course of riding bucking
> ponies, and assist at the branding of a lot of Texas steer.[48]

It is not surprising that Roosevelt chose to pose in his cowboy
outfit for a photograph to serve as the frontispiece for his *Hunting Trips of a Ranchman* in 1885. For to him, then as later, the
big sombrero, the chaps, the boots, the spurs, and the six-shooter
symbolized true red-blooded Americanism. Roosevelt had seen
Mexicans, Negroes, and Indians among the cowboys,[49] but the
men he worked with were overwhelmingly from good Teutonic
stock, uncontaminated by the blood of "inferior" races. In an
environment that as a condition of survival demanded "self-
reliance, hardihood, and . . . instant decision,"[50] unweakened by

[46] Ibid., p. 173.

[47] Ibid., p. 169.

[48] Ibid., p. 156; Pringle, *Theodore Roosevelt*, p. 97.

[49] Theodore Roosevelt, *Ranch Life and the Hunting Trail* (New York,
1902), p. 11; Hagedorn, *Roosevelt in the Bad Lands*, p. 264.

[50] *Autobiography*, p. 96.

luxury or overrefinement, the cowboys would not "submit tamely to an insult," and "had no overwrought fear of shedding blood." They possessed "few of the emasculated, milk-and-water moralities admired by the pseudo-philanthropist," but they possessed, "to a very high degree, the stern manly virtues that are invaluable to a nation."[51] There were no cosmopolitans or expatriates among them. Responding automatically to their spiritual racial heritage, they did what was right without agonizing metaphysical speculation.

Roosevelt was proud to have been one of them, and freely acknowledged his indebtedness to them. He wrote Gilder in 1886: "I have been a part of all I describe [in *The Wilderness Hunter*]; I have seen the things and done them; I have herded my own cattle; I have killed my own food; I have shot bears, captured horse thieves, and 'stood off' Indians."[52]

Upon his first contact with the cowboys Roosevelt saw them as potential soldiers and planned in the event of war to enlist a regiment of them. The war was longer in coming than he wished, but it eventually came. His adventure with the Rough Riders, three-fourths of whom, he said "had at some time or other been cowboys or else small stockmen,"[53] made him President. He acknowledged his debt.

"Not only did the men and women whom I met in the cow country quite unconsciously help me, by the insight which working and living with them enabled me to get into the mind and soul of the average American of the right type, but they helped me in another way. I made up my mind that the men were just the kind whom it would be well to have with me if ever it became necessary to go to war. When the Spanish War came, I gave this thought practical realization."[54]

---

[51] *Ranch Life and the Hunting Trail*, p. 55.
[52] *Letters*, vol. 1, pp. 143–144.
[53] *Letters*, vol. 2, p. 833.
[54] *Autobiography*, p. 122.

Upon the death of McKinley, Mark Hanna is reputed to have been weeping over the loss of his friend and cursing the fact that "that damned cowboy is the President of the United States." But what nettled Roosevelt was that Hanna treated him like a boy and called him Teddy.[55] There is a vast difference between *boy* and *cowboy*.

If at home and abroad Roosevelt symbolized the American of the first decade of this century, the cowboy shared largely in that symbolism.

[55] Pringle, *Theodore Roosevelt*, p. 239.

13. How Will Boatright Made Bits and Spurs (1970)

I N his excellent article on tire shrinking, which furnished half the title of the Texas Folklore Publication for 1968, E. J. Rissman described in lucid and interesting detail one of the techniques of a professional smith some fifty or sixty years ago.[1] I shall attempt to deal similarly with the making of bits and spurs, not by a professional like the famous Petmecky of Austin, whose Petmaker spurs were known and valued from the Rio Grande to the Columbia, but by one who would now be called a hobbyist working at home.

But first a word about the home blacksmith shop as an institution in the ranch country of my boyhood. Such shops were to be

NOTE: Originally published in *Journal of American Folklore* 83 (January–March 1970): 77–80. Version of a paper read at the meeting of the Texas Folklore Society, Dallas, Texas, April 4, 1969.

[1] "The Tire Shrinker," in *Tire Shrinker to Dragster*, edited by Wilson M. Hudson (Austin, 1958), pp. 3–9.

found on most of the ranches except those within easy reach of a professional. Easy reach in those days was not very far. To travel by buggy the twelve miles between our ranch house and Mr. Craddock's shop in Sanco, Texas, required about two hours. Thus four hours would be consumed on the trip alone, in addition to the time required to sharpen a plow or shoe a horse. You could save time and money by buying equipment and doing your work at home.

The larger items, which could be had at the hardware or general stores in Colorado City, Sweetwater, and San Angelo, or from Sears and Roebuck, consisted of an anvil, a vise, and a forge. Everybody knows the shape of an anvil, but perhaps two features should be mentioned. Between the main surface and the horn, and somewhat lower, was a plane faced with soft steel. This was to avoid dulling your chisel when you wished to cut through a hot bar or rod. In the wing of the anvil were two holes, one about an inch square for holding chisels and dollies, and the other smaller and round, over which you placed anything you wished to punch a hole in (fig.1). And in those days before rural electrification you never did anything with hacksaw or drill that you could do with chisel or punch.

The vise (fig. 2) was not like those commonly seen in garages and machine shops today. It had to be heavy and made of high quality steel, capable of absorbing hard blows on a piece of hot iron. It was securely mounted to a sturdy bench whose legs

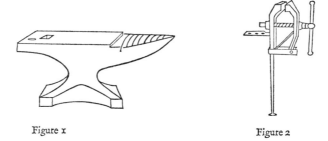

Figure 1   Figure 2

were posts well anchored in the ground. To save the bench from the impact of heavy pounding, one leg of the vise extended to the ground and rested on a short post also well anchored.

One of our neighbors had a forge with a bellows like the one the elder Rissmann first used. It was the only one of its kind I ever saw in operation. The ones commonly used within my memory were made of cast iron and equipped with a lever- or crank-operated fan, which supplied a continuous blast of air (fig. 3). The fuel, purchasable at the hardware and general

Figure 3

stores under the label of blacksmith's coal, was an egg-sized anthracite packaged in hundred-pound bags.

In the shop, of course, would be a variety of hand tools: sledges of different weights, ball-peen hammers of different sizes, punches, brace and bits for metal and wood, taps and dies for cutting threads, files of various shapes ranging from flat bastards to round rat tails; and of course a set of farrier's tools: hammer, pinchers, rasp, and hoof knife.

As I have implied, the home shop was primarily a utilitarian institution. But among ranch people there would be some who made things just for the pleasure of making them. One of these was Will Boatright, my brother and my senior by twenty years, who so far as I know never asked for or accepted money for a bit or a spur. At any time I saw smoke coming out of the shop indicating that a fire had been started, or heard the click-click of the rachet on the forge or the ring of a hammer on the anvil, I rushed out to see what was going on. Will might be making something, and if he needed a third hand to hold one of the pieces he was welding, I was not unhappy to oblige him.

But there was no welding to do when he made bits or spurs. Bits were often made of three pieces, a mouth piece and two side pieces, and spurs of two pieces, the heel band and the shank. Whether Will used a one-piece design because he thought it superior or whether it was to show his skill, I do not know.

If he wished to make bits, he would go out back of the shop where all worn-out implements were parked and where all discarded objects containing usable metal were piled, and select a steel rod a half an inch in diameter and eighteen to twenty inches long. First he would heat the rod in the middle to a glowing red and bend the port (fig. 4). The port extended upward

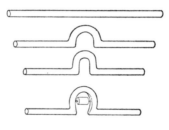

Figure 4

and could be brought to bear on the tender roof of the horse's mouth. It was a device borrowed from the vaqueros and thought by some of the Englishmen who came to the American West to be barbarously cruel. If they remained a while they learned better. I have seen more abuse of this bit in the movies than I ever saw or heard about among cow people.

We had on our ranch at one time a horse named Joe. Joe was fast and alert, had an easy gait and a head full of cow sense. His flaw came from an excess of one of his virtues. He had too much energy, and the work being done did not always provide a sufficient outlet. Then he might grasp the bit in his teeth and go for a run. I could have jerked the bit loose and brought the port into play, but I knew better. Neither my father nor his neighbors would tolerate jerking, and a man who rode a sore-mouthed horse would be thought capable of beating his wife. I would pull steadily on the reins until Joe's jaws got tired, then I would keep a tight rein, turning the port outward so he could not clamp the bit, until he quieted down.

Ports were of different sizes. Will made his about an inch and a half high.

If he wished to supply a cricket, or taster, as it was sometimes called, he would do it at this stage. He would punch small holes, say the size of a large nail, in each side of the port. He would then make a corrugated copper cylinder three-eighths of an inch in diameter. The cylinder could be made by wrapping a piece of heavy-gauge sheet copper around a small bolt. The edges had to be smoothly joined with no sharp edges left. The cylinder was inserted in the port so as to rotate on a nail serving as an axis. The nail would be cut so that the ends did not extend quite to the surface of the port, and the holes would be closed (fig.4).

If the port was for the control of the horse, the cricket was for his pleasure. It served no other purpose. There were some who believed that the horse's pleasure came from the taste of the copper, and to them the device was a taster. I am not of that school. The bridle that came with the saddle I received from my father on my seventh birthday had a cricket bit, and as I rode Old Paint at a walk or fox trot, he rolled the cricket with his tongue, making it chirp. I am sure it was the sound that pleased him. I enjoyed it too.

The port made and the cricket, if any, installed, Will would next flatten the ends of the rod somewhat and split them with a hot chisel, that is, one thinner and sharper than the cold chisel used for cutting unheated metal (fig. 5). The splits would ex-

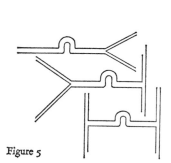

Figure 5

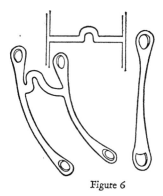

Figure 6

tend to slightly more than two and a half inches from the center
of the port, so that the mouthpiece would be five inches long.
This was standard. A small horse could wear the bit with comfort, and a horse too big for it should be pulling a beer wagon.

When he had made the splits, Will would screw the mouthpiece firmly in the vise, bend the ends to a right angle, and
hammer until all the evidence of the cut was gone and until the
sides extended a little beyond the mouthpiece. When both sides
had been thus treated, he cut off the excess metal. The sidepieces
would be six or seven inches in length, the part below the mouthpiece longer than the part above. This was necessary to establish
a center of gravity so the port would remain upright in the
horse's mouth. Then Will would take the work to the anvil and
flatten and shape the sides. He would cut a slot near the end of
each sidepiece and drive a punch in the slot and enlarge it until
it would go over the point of the anvil for final shaping (fig. 6).
When the forging was all done, he would put the bit in the vise
and smooth all surfaces with files. Then he would heat the entire bit to a uniform heat and plunge it into water for tempering,
after which he would give it a final polishing.

To make a spur he would begin with a piece of steel with a
diameter a little larger than that for a bit. He would split it and

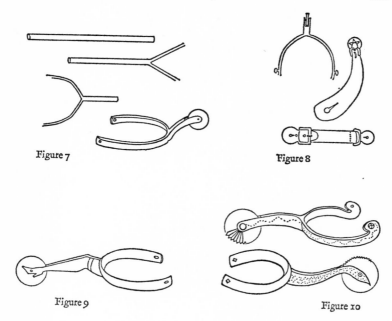

Figure 7

Figure 8

Figure 9

Figure 10

shape the heel band on the horn of the anvil (fig. 7). The shank would require considerable forging, since it had to be brought down to the proper size. He used a hacksaw to make a slit for the rowel, which on his spurs had small blunt teeth. The buttons for the leathers could be made by filing off the square shoulder of a carriage bolt and using the head (fig. 8).

There were two patterns of spurs used widely enough in our country to qualify as folk designs: the goose neck and the lady's leg (fig. 9). Will Boatright made neither of these. Nor did he overload his bits and spurs with silver ornamentation as the Californians, even before Tom Mix, were wont to do. Will was not a phrase maker and it would never have occurred to him to say, "Form follows function," (fig. 10), but I think Louis Henry Sullivan would have been pleased with his products.

A SELECTED BIBLIOGRAPHY
OF MODY BOATRIGHT'S WORKS

BOOKS

Accuracy in Thinking. New York: Farrar and Rinehart, 1938.

Folk Laughter on the American Frontier. New York: Macmillan, 1949.

Folklore of the Oil Industry. Dallas: Southern Methodist University Press, 1963.

Gib Morgan: Minstrel of the Oil Fields. Illustrated by Betty Boatright. Austin: Texas Folklore Society, 1945.

Tales from the Derrick Floor: A People's History of the Oil Industry. (with William A. Owens). Garden City, New York: Doubleday and Company, 1970.

Tall Tales from Texas Cow Camps. Dallas: Southwest Press, 1934.

ARTICLES

"The American Myth Rides the Range: Owen Wister's Man on Horseback." *Southwest Review* 36 (summer 1951): 157–162.

"The American Rodeo." *American Quarterly* 16 (summer 1964): 195–202.

"The Art of Tall Lying." *Southwest Review* 33 (August 1949): 357–362.

"Aunt Cordie's Ax and Other Motifs in Oil." In *Folk Travelers*, pp. 75–85. Publications of the Texas Folklore Society, no. 25. Dallas: Southern Methodist University Press, 1953.

"Backwoods Belles." In *Backwoods to Border*, pp. 61–78. Publications of the Texas Folklore Society, no. 18. Dallas: Southern Methodist University Press, 1943.

"The Beginnings of Cowboy Fiction." *Southwest Review* 51 (winter 1966): 11–28.

"Birds and Beasts." *Texas Monthly* 4 (November 1929): 450–457.

"Comic Exempla of the Pioneer Pulpit." In *Coyote Wisdom*, pp. 155–168. Publications of the Texas Folklore Society, no. 14. Dallas: Southern Methodist University Press, 1938.

"The Cowboy Enters the Movies." In *The Sunny Slopes of Long Ago*, pp. 51–69. Publications of the Texas Folklore Society, no. 33. Dallas: Southern Methodist University Press, 1966.

"Cowboy Yarns of Wind and Weather." *Texas Monthly* 5 (May 1930): 412–417.

"Demonology in the Novels of Sir Walter Scott." The University of Texas *Studies in English* 14 (1934): 75–88.

"The Devil's Grotto." In *Texas and Southwest Lore*, pp. 102–107. Publications of the Texas Folklore Society, no. 6. Austin: Texas Folklore Society, 1927.

"The Family Saga as a Form of Folklore." In *The Family Saga and Other Phases of American Folklore*, pp.1–19. Urbana: University of Illinois Press, 1958.

"Folklore in a Literate Society." In *Madstones and Twisters*, pp. 45–51. Publications of the Texas Folklore Society, no. 28. Dallas: Southern Methodist University Press, 1958.

"The Formula in Cowboy Fiction and Drama." *Western Folklore* 28 (April 1969): 136–145.

"Frontier Humor: Despairing or Buoyant?" *Southwest Review* 27 (spring 1942): 320–334.

"The Genius of Pecos Bill." *Southwest Review* 14 (July 1929): 418–428.

"The Geologist in the Oil Field." *Southwest Review* 46 (autumn 1961): 311–319.

"How Will Boatright Made Bits and Spurs." *Journal of American Folklore* 83 (January–March 1970): 77–80.

"Law and Laughter on the Frontier." *Southwest Review* 30 (winter 1954): 175–181.

"The Literature of the Southwest." In *Regional Culture: A Sympo-*

sium, pp. 11–18. Alpine, Texas: West Texas Historical and Scientific Society, 1953.

"The Morality Play on Hoseback: Tom Mix." In *Tire Shrinker to Dragster*, pp. 63–71. Publications of the Texas Folklore Society, no. 34. Austin: Encino Press, 1968.

"The Myth of Frontier Individualism." *Southwestern Social Science Quarterly* 22 (July 1941): 12–32.

"Oil by Hook or Crook." *Southwest Review* 31 (spring 1946): 122–128.

"Oil on the Wastelands." *Texas Quarterly* 1 (winter 1958): 7–16.

"The Oil Promoter as Trickster." In *Singers and Story Tellers*, pp. 76–91. Publications of the Texas Folklore Society, no. 30. Dallas: Southern Methodist University Press, 1961.

"On the Nature of Myth." *Southwest Review* 39 (spring 1954): 131–136.

"The Petroleum Geologist: A Folk Image." In *The Golden Log*, pp. 58–72. Publications of the Texas Folklore Society, no. 31. Dallas: Southern Methodist University Press, 1962.

"Pizenous Windies." *Texas Monthly* 4 (August 1929): 41–49.

"Scott's Theory and Practice Concerning the Use of the Supernatural in Prose Fiction." *Publications of the Modern Language Association* 50 (March 1935): 235–261.

"The Tall Tale in Texas." *South Atlantic Quarterly* 30 (July 1931): 271–279.

"Theodore Roosevelt, Social Darwinism, and the Cowboy." *Texas Quarterly* 7 (winter 1964): 11–20.

"The Western Bad Man as Hero." In *Mesquite and Willow*, pp. 96–104. Publications of the Texas Folklore Society, no. 27. Dallas: Southern Methodist University Press, 1957.

"Whitman and Hegel." The University of Texas *Studies in English* 9 (1929): 134–150.

"Witchcraft in the Novels of Sir Walter Scott." The University of Texas *Studies in English* 13 (1933): 95–112.

INDEX

Adamic, Louis: and Yugoslavian weddings, 117
Adams, Brooks: 170
Adams, Henry: 165
Adams, James Truslow: as proponent of myth of frontier individualism, 14
Alger, Horatio: as example of myth of faithful apprentice, 84
American Dream, Great: shattering of, 85
animal stories. SEE family saga
anti-horse-thief associations: in Nebraska, 22; in Oklahoma, 22
anvil: 180
archetypal stories: in oil folklore, 92. SEE ALSO trickster
Associated Advertising Clubs of the World: vigilance committee of, 155
Austin, Mary: and folk groups, 118
Austin, Stephen F.: as leader of pioneer settlers, 16
ax. SEE motifs in oil folklore

Bacon, Francis: 71
Baird, Robert: on oratory, 52
Baker, Jim: as example of hero, 78
Baldwin, Joseph G.: 71
Bancroft, George: on influence of American form of government, 51–52
Beadle and Adams: dime novel publishers, 163
Beard, Charles: on rugged individualism, 15
Beard, Charles and Mary: on settlers, 16
Beaver, Tony: tales of, compared to Gib Morgan's, 63
Beckwith, Martha: on folk tale, 125
Benchley, Nathaniel: on family lore, 126–127
Benchley, Robert: story in biography of, 126
Beowulf: 70
Besant, Sir Walter: 168
Big Lake Field: and million-dollar drink, 102–103
bits, bridle: making of, 182–184
Blair, Walter: 65; as contributing to clustering of folk tales, 77
Boatright, Elizabeth Keefer: xv
Boatright, Mody C.: as folklorist, vii–ix, xix–xxiii; biographical information on, xi–xviii; as editor, xii–xiii; and oral history, xii; as administrator, xiii–xvii; on University admissions policy, xv; and the cowboy, xvii, xx–xxi; as letter

writer, xviii; publishing career of, xix; interests of, xix–xxiii; and frontier folk life, xxi; and tall tale, xxi; and oil folklore, xxi–xxii; and folklorist in contemporary society, xxii–xxiii; and folklore collecting, xxii; and folk crafts, xxii

Boatright, Will: as folk craftsman, 179–185

Bolus, Ovid: as tall tale teller, 71

Bon, Gustave Le. SEE Le Bon, Gustave

Boone, Daniel: as land agent, 16; as frontiersman, 40; as example of mythological symbol, 112

Boyd, Ernest: on rugged individualism, 14

Braddy, Haldeen: and new ax story, 94

Bradford, Roark. SEE John Henry

Brer Rabbit: as trickster, 145–146

Brewer, J. Mason: quoted, 76

Bridger, Jim: 56

bridle bits. SEE bits, bridle

Brooks, Van Wyck: and despair of frontier humor, 39

Buffalo Bill: 164

"Buffalo Skinners": and frontier labor relations, 29–30

Bunyan, Paul: compared to cowboy hero, 4; as hero type, 5; compared to Gib Morgan, 62; publicizing of, 65; supplants Gib Morgan, 66; and dissemination of folklore, 122

Butler, P. D.: on communal cattle gathering, 18–19

Carnegie, Andrew: and gospel of stewardship, 85; and Theodore Roosevelt, 168n.

Carr, John: on communal building of church, 19

Carson, Kit: 40, 56; as mythological symbol, 112

Carter, Nick: 164

Cartwright, Peter: on clustering of folk tales, 77; as person about whom tales cluster, 143

cattlemen's associations: 27–28

Cinderella: 146

claim clubs: 23–26

Clemens, Samuel: on pilots' wages, 32; on pilots' organization, 32. SEE ALSO Mark Twain

Cline, Walter: on lucky breakdown story, 97–99

Colorado City, Texas: 180

Communist Manifesto: as revolutionary myth, 114–115

Comstock, Chris: 164

Cook, Dr. Frederick A.: 152, 155, 159–160

cowboy: xvii, xx–xxi; as hero of tall tale, 4; labor relations of, 30–31; prevalence of, 80–81; as popular hero, 81–82; and dime novels, 82; as Wister's faithful apprentice, 84–85; and adult readers, 164. SEE ALSO Owen Wister; Theodore Roosevelt

Cox, S. S.: and parody of Joseph C. Guild, 54–55; on humor, 55

Cox, Seymour E. J. SEE Dr. Frederick A. Cook

creeping socialism: as example of personified mythological symbol, 112

cricket: of bridle bit, 183

Crockett, David: 5, 40; as frontier magistrate, 20; and loss of gristmill, 48; on effect of steamboat on frontier language, 58; compared to Gib Morgan, 62; as legendary hero, 63; public recognition of, 65; as hero about whom tales cluster, 77

Croy, Homer: and James family saga, 125

Davis, E. J.: and range laws, 34–35

Deadwood Dick: 164

de Tormes, Lazarillo. SEE Tormes, Lazarillo de

De Voto, Bernard: on frontier humor, 39

DeWees, W. E.: 128

Dick, Everett: on unwritten law of frontier, 21

Dilke, Charles Wentworth: on claim clubs, 24; on effect of Western terrain on thought and humor, 55–56

dime novels: 163–164

Dobie, J. Frank: vii, xiv, 3; on tall tale, 73–74; on panther stories, 131n.; story from childhood of, 132–133

Doggett, Jim: quoted, 130

Dorson, Richard: delineation of folk hero by, 63; on journalists and folklore, 122

Doutté, Edmond: and definition of myth, 107

dreams. SEE family saga

Duarte family: 140

Duncan, Bob: and new ax story, 94

Durkheim, Emile: and definition of myth, 107–108

Duval, Jon C.: 135n.

Dwight, Timothy: on reasons for going to frontier, 127

Eastman, Max: on frontier humor, 39

Eisenhower, Dwight: as mythological symbol, 112

Everett, Edward: on American form of government, 51

family saga: as family stories, 124; and social values, 125–127; animal stories in, 130–135; role of dreams in, 135–139; missed fortune stories in, 139–141; as sources of folklore, 142–144

"Famous Oil Firms": quoted, 148

Fink, Mike: 62, 65; as example of hero about whom tales cluster, 77

Finley, J. B.: on settlers in Ohio Valley, 17

Flint, Timothy: on unconscious poetry in pioneer, 57; on effect of steamboat on frontier language, 57–58; on frontier literature, 70

folk: concepts of, 118–120

folk archetype. SEE trickster

folk crafts: xxii; sources of, 117–118; changes in, 120; emergence of new, 120–121; home blacksmithing as, 179–185

folk hero: qualities of, 81. SEE ALSO Pecos Bill; Gib Morgan; Owen Wister; cowboy

folklore: concerns of, in past, 118; dissemination of, in literate society, 121–122; creation of, in literate society, 122–123. SEE ALSO family saga; motifs in oil folklore; tall tale; trickster

folklorists: xxii–xxiii

folk tales: clustering of, 77–78; about real persons, 143. SEE ALSO Pecos Bill; Gib Morgan; family saga; cowboy; tall tale

folkways: of pioneer, communal nature of, 16–21; as source of law, 20–21; and lack of theoretical economics, 36–37; in contemporary society, 117; in commercial society, 121. SEE ALSO Theodore Roosevelt

forge: 181

Fowler, S. L.: and lucky breakdown story, 96–99

Frazer, James: on primacy of ritual, 113

free enterprise: as personified mythological symbol, 112
free silver. SEE Owen Wister
frontier: xxi; freebooters on, 15;
protective associations on, 21–23;
mining claim laws on, 22–23; and
cattlemen, 25; and cattle industry,
27–29; labor relations on, 29–32;
range cattle laws on, 34–35; regulation of railroads on, 35–36; attitude toward defeat on, 47–48; optimism and democracy on, 48–50;
and manifest destiny, 50–57; effect
of steamboats on, 58–59; railroads
on, 59; special interests on, 59. SEE
ALSO folkways; pioneers
frontier humor: belief in despair of,
39–40; evidence to support despair of, 41–47; reasons for not accepting despair of, 47–60. SEE ALSO
folkways; pioneers
frontier individualism, myth of:
chief proponents of, 13–15; mutuality as refutation of, 16–20;
self-regulation as refutation of,
20–29; labor movements as refutation of, 29–34; range laws as
refutation of, 34–35; railroad legislation as refutation of, 35–36; reasons for acceptance of, 37. SEE
ALSO folkways; frontier; pioneers
frontier literature: lack of adequate,
69–70. SEE ALSO tall tale

Garland, Hamlin: on measures
against horse stealing, 22; on frontier literature, 70
George, Henry: Theodore Roosevelt's opinion of, 165
ghost dance. SEE Wovoka
Glimp famil saga: 131
Goodnight, Charles: on branding of
stray cattle, 26; and Panhandle
Stock Association, 28; and failure

of banking business, 48; mentioned, 40, 56
Gould, Jay: and labor disputes, 33;
119
group migration: 18
Guerra family: 140–142
Guild, Joseph C.: and spread-eagle
oratory, 53–54

Hagedorn, Herbert: quoted, 169
Hall, Captain Basil: 42
Hall, Judge James: as interpreter of
frontiersman, 41; on frontier lit-
erature, 70
Hammet, Samuel Adams: 127–128
Hanna, Mark: 178
Harriman, E. H.: and social regula-
tion and pioneer ideals, 14
Harte, Bret: and frontier humor, 70
Hay, John: letter to, 164; Theodore
Roosevelt's opinion of, 165
Henry, John: as creator of Roark
Bradford, 78
Henry, O.: realism of, 73
Herskovits, Melville: on secular
rites, 113
Hoover, Herbert: and rugged indi-
vidualism, 14
Hornsby, Ruben: as early settler,
135–136
Houston, Sam: as person about
whom stories cluster, 143
humor: theories of, 46–47. SEE ALSO
frontier humor
Huntington, Collis: 119

Jackson, Andrew: as person about
whom stories cluster, 143
Jackson, Gabriel Asbury: 10
James, Henry: 165
James, Jesse: folklore about, 125
James, W. S.: and understatement,
72–73
Joiner, Dad: as oil promoter, 147

Jones, Casey: 119

Kittredge, George Lyman: xii
Kluckhohn, Clyde: and definition of myth, 107
Kremlin: as personified mythological symbol, 112
Krupp, Hyman: as organizer of Sun Oil Company, 99

law, frontier. SEE frontier; folkways
Lawrence, Adam: 130; family saga of, 133–135
Le Bon, Gustave: 168n., 170
Lee, Robert A.: 153
Lee, Robert E.: 153
Lincoln, Abraham: Gettysburg Address, 52; as example of person about whom stories cluster, 143
Lodge, Henry Cabot: 168n.
Lomax, John A.: vii, 3
Lorimer, Horace: 90
lucky breakdown. SEE motifs in oil folklore
Lynd, Robert: and theory of laughter, 46–47

McClesky, John and Cordie: 92–95, 102, 104
Mackay, Alexander: on behavior of Englishmen on frontier, 41; on pride of frontiersmen in democracy, 48–49
Malinowski, Bronislaw: and definition of myth, 108
Malthusianism: American rejection of, 56
manifest destiny: as characteristic of an age, 68. SEE ALSO frontier
Marryat, Captain Frederick: and encroachment on mining claim, 23; mock fight staged for, 42
Meine, Franklin J.: and Mike Fink, 65; and clustering of folk tales, 77

Melville, Herman: on whalers' wages, 31–32; and belief in democracy, 50–51
Mencken, H. L.: 43
Milburn, W. H.: 43; and frontier speech making, 56–57
million-dollar drink. SEE motifs in oil folklore
mining claim laws. SEE frontier
missed fortune stories. SEE family saga
Mix, Tom: 185
Morgan, Gib: as real person, 61; compared to other folk heroes, 62–63; as folk hero, 63; and nature of comic myths, 63–65; borrowed tales of, 65; discovery of, 65–66; supplanted by Paul Bunyan, 66; as symbol of era, 66–67; and exaggeration in tall tale, 72
motifs: and family saga, 124
motifs in oil folklore: typical, 92–105; and the new ax, 92–95; and the lucky breakdown, 95–102; and the million-dollar drink, 102–104; dissemination of, 104; development of, 104–105
Muir, Andrew Forest. SEE Nathaniel Benchley
Mumford, Lewis: 39, 57
Munchausen: and the cowboy, 4; and Gib Morgan tales, 65
myth: concept of, 106–107; definitions of, 107–109; theme and function of, 109; of racial superiority, 109; and desire for dignity, 109–111; and desire for security, 109–111; assumptions of universal, 110–111; and mythological symbols, 112; and personified mythological symbols, 112; and ritual, 113; conservative nature of, 114–115; revolutionary nature of, 114–115; in literate society, 115. SEE

ALSO cowboy; frontier individual-ism, myth of

Neiman-Marcus: as source of folk custom, 117
New York Times: on oil advertise-ments, 155

Ochiltree, Tom: on lying, 71
Odyssey: 70
Oedipus: as myth without ritual, 113
oil company names: 152–153
oil folklore. SEE motifs in oil folk-lore; trickster
oil promoter: definition of, 147; ridi-cule of, 148–149; amounts swin-dled by, 160–161. SEE ALSO tricks of oil promoters; trickster
O'Reilly, Edward: and clustering of folk tales, 77
Osgood, Ernest Staples: and misin-terpretation of frontier, 20

Paine, Albert Bigelow: and despair of frontier humor, 39–40
"Panther in Pursuit" stories: 131–133
"Panther on the Roof" stories: 131–132
Parrington, Vernon Louis: on fron-tier social protest, 14–15
Pecos Bill: as cowboy hero, 5, 62; birth of, 5; and mosquitoes, 6–7; and panther, 8; death of, 9–11; men killed by, 11–12; as hero about whom tales cluster, 77–78
Pentagon: as personified mythologi-cal symbol, 112
Perry, George Sessions: on new ax motif, 94
Pickrell, Frank: and lucky break-down motif, 100–102; and million-dollar drink motif, 102–103
pioneers: and absentee ownership,

35; and regulation of private en-terprise, 36; and private property, 37. SEE ALSO frontier
Pomeroy, Samuel C.: and spread-eagle oratory, 52–53
Populism. SEE Owen Wister
port: of bridle bit, 182–183
Post, Emily: as source of folk cus-tom, 117
Pound, Ezra: and American experi-ment, 60
Prometheus: 111
protective associations. SEE frontier; anti-horse-thief associations

railroad legislation. SEE frontier
railroads: frontier humor about, 59
range cattle industry. SEE frontier
range laws. SEE frontier
Ranger, Texas: oil field at, 92–95
Rangers, Texas. SEE Texas Rangers
Reuther, Walter: as example of American folk, 119
Richards, I. A.: and realms of opin-ion, 109
Rissman, E. J.: 179
Rister, Carl Coke: quoted, 160–161
ritual: contemporary, 113–114; na-ture of, 114. SEE ALSO myth
Robb, John S.: 55
Robin Hood: as folk hero, 122
Roosevelt, Franklin D.: as mytho-logical symbol, 112
Roosevelt, Captain Nicholas: and shallow-draft steamer, 58
Roosevelt, Theodore: as mythological symbol, 112; and social Darwin-ism, 163–178; and ideals of Ameri-cans, 164–165; and manly virtues, 165; and men of action, 165; and opinions of contemporaries, 165; and legal procedures, 165–166; and lynch law, 166; and folkways, 166; on passing of open range,

167; racial views of, 168–169; and criminals, 169–170; and soldierly virtues, 171–173; acceptance of, among cowboys, 173–177; on cowboys as potential soldiers, 177. SEE ALSO Owen Wister

Russell, Charles M.: and understatement, 73

Rust, John: on McClesky ax story, 94–95; on dreams, 137–139

Rysan, Josef: and definition of myth, 107–108

San Angelo, Texas: 180

Santa Rita. SEE motifs in oil folklore

Saturday Evening Post: as publisher of cowboy stories, 80; as voice of businessman, 90

Sears and Roebuck: 180

Sellers, Beriah: as typical frontiersman, 47

Shephard, Esther: as publicist for Paul Bunyan, 66

Siringo, Charles: as contemporary of Owen Wister, 82

Slick, Sam: 147

Smalley, E. V.: on working of cattlemen's associations, 27

Smiley, Alfred W.: 150

Smith, Henry Nash: on myth and symbol, 112

Smithwick, Noah: on mutual protection on frontier, 17

social Darwinism: and businessmen, 87; as example of universal myth, 110. SEE ALSO Theodore Roosevelt; Owen Wister

socialism. SEE Owen Wister

Social Statics: as example of conservative myth, 114

Solms-Braunfels, Prince Carl: as leader of frontier settlers, 16

Speck, Ernest B.: vii

Spencer, Herbert: as prophet of social Darwinism, 85; and Theodore Roosevelt, 168–170

Spider Woman: 111

spread-eagle oratory: as expression of optimism, 52–55; as characteristic of an age, 66

spurs: 179, 184–185

steamboats. SEE frontier

Stevens, James: as publicist of Paul Bunyan, 66

Stewart, Donald Ogden: on theory of humor, 47

Street and Smith: as dime novel publishers, 163

Sullivan, Louis Henry: 185

Sumner, William Graham: quoted, 86

Sweetwater, Texas: 180

Swindletop: 160

Tait, Samuel W., Jr.: on prevalence of lucky breakdown motif, 96

tale types: 124

tall tale: xxi; cowboy use of, 3–4; as form of American folk humor, 68; as popular literature, 68–71; as indigenous art form, 71; reasons for telling, 71; characteristics of, 71–77; kind of exaggeration in, 71–72; understatement in, 72–73; realistic basis of, 73–74; circumstantial detail in, 74; structure of, 74–77. SEE ALSO Gib Morgan

Taylor, Buck: 164

Texas Folklore Society: vii–viii, xii

Texas Rangers: 141–142

Thoms, William John: as coiner of *folk-lore*, 118

Tormes, Lazarillo de: 146

tricks of oil promoters: and well salting, 149–151; and verbal skill, 151–160; and names for oil companies, 152–153; and planted news stories, 152–154; and oil journals,